Dro

Drop Dead Gorgeous
Book 4: Crystal Creek Mysteries

By M. Sue Alexander

M. Sue Alexander

M. Sue Alexander

This book is a work of fiction. Names and characters in the story are a product of the author's imagination. Any resemblance to actual persons, living or dead, events or locales, is coincidental. Should you purchase a copy of this book without a cover, be aware this book may be stolen property and neither the publisher nor the author has received payment for a "stripped book."

Book 4: Crystal Creek Mysteries
Drop Dead Gorgeous
FIRST EDITION 2022, USA
SUZANDER PUBLISHING
Copyright © 2022 by M. Sue Alexander

All rights reserved by author. No part of this book may be reproduced in any form, either by electronic or mechanical means, including information storage and retrieval systems, without obtaining written permission from the publisher, except by a reviewer who may quote brief passages in a review. Scripture quotations are from *The Living Bible*. Copyright © 1971, Tyndale House Publishers; Wheaton, Illinois 60187, and used by permission. All rights reserved.

Book Cover by Christine Roszak

View M. Sue's Website and Facebook Page
www.msuealexanderbooks.com

Contents

The average business owner has a better chance of winning the lottery than hiring a great online marketing partner 1

Why we wrote this book 3

Hard Truth Number One: You won't succeed long term without outside help 5

Hard Truth Number Two: Winners focus on ROI - not cost 7

Hard Truth Number Three: A bad contract guarantees failure .. 11

Hard Truth Number Four: You go to bed with the salesperson but wake up with the account manager 13

Hard Truth Number Five: Bad companies don't come with warning labels 17

Hard Truth Number Six: The worst advice comes with good intentions 21

Hard Truth Number Seven: Even great partners need to be managed 25

About the Authors 30

Want a Free Assessment? 32

The average business owner has a better chance of winning the lottery than hiring a great online marketing partner

Surprised? So were we... until we started talking to other business owners about their experiences. Having struggled to find quality partners in our own businesses, we began surveying other business owners across the country three years ago and the stories they told all had a similar theme:

"I hired this Internet marketing company and paid them for six months to get me Google traffic and I don't even know what they did. They kept sending me reports that showed my traffic going up, but my sales didn't budge. I'm not sure they did any work at all."

or

"I've hired three different companies in the last two years and each one comes in with a great pitch and a good story about how they're going to help me, but I just never see any results. After a couple of months I barely hear from them; I get a few emails and canned reports and that's it. The only time they seem to do anything is when I complain."

or

"I hired a company to do all of our social media and paid search and things were great for a couple of months... but then deteriorated quickly. They never asked any questions and I could see from my account that they weren't making any updates. The social content they posted was riddled with errors and obviously not written by a native English speaker. It was a huge waste of money."

Series Titles by Author

Resurrection Dawn 2014 Series
Book 1: Resurrection Dawn 2014   *Book 2:* The Christian Fugitive
Book 3: Rebels in Paradise   *Book 4:* Veil of Lies
Book 5: The Anointing   *Book 6:* Countdown to Justice
Book 7: All Rise   *Book 8:* Unlikely Suspect
Book 9: Lethal Snapshot   *Book 10:* Purgatory
Book 11: April Fool's Day   *Book 12:* Reign of Errors

Time of Jacob's Trouble
Book 1: The Four Horsemen   *Book 2:* Beast
Book 3: Witness   *Book 4:* The Word
Book 5: Judgment   *Book 6:* Deceiver
Book 7: False Prophet   *Book 8:* Satan
Book 9: The Image
Book 10: Jesus the Appearance

Crystal Creek Mysteries
Book 1: Two Dead on Crystal Creek
Book 2: Poison Tea
Book 3: A Latte to Die For
Book 4: Drop Dead Gorgeous

Independent Titles
Adam's Bones
Encounters of the God-Kind
Grandma's Coming (children's book)
Out of Time: The Vanderbilt Incident
The Forum
The Minister's Haunting
Tomorrow's Promise

1

Wednesday, July 5

THE HISSING OF AIR through the AC vents in Captain Marilyn Colbert's office located on the third floor of the Columbia Police Department is foretelling as she addresses the lead detective. Marilyn's mood is as dark as her skin, her gaze as sharp as the cutting edge of a razor, her demeanor serious and urgent.

"Have they found her yet?" She refers to Dorothy Jean Powell.

"No, ma'am," Detective Galena Chico respectively replies.

Marilyn nods, also foretelling. "We know who the Vic is."

"Yes, ma'am."

The captain refers to Dominick Raphael Karensky, the great-grandson of the deceased Alexander Karensky, head of a Provisional Government run by Russian progressives in the 20th century. The spy agency Dom belonged to is SVR, or the Foreign Intelligence Service of the Russian Federation, directed under President Vladimir Putin. SVR's operative goal is to penetrate the U.S. government and learn it's secrets in order to convert a democratic regime to a socialist one.

More recently, Putin had waged a war in Ukraine to conquer territory. Believing the country belonged to Russia, he desired control of the huge amounts of grain grown in the country. Something the European world needed to avoid a hunger crisis. Less socialistic, Putin had become a cruel rogue dictator taking no enemy survivors.

SVR's tactics were brutal and uncompromising.

"Is that all you have to say, Detective Chico?" Marilyn taps her ballpoint pen on her calendar, stumped by Dorothy's disappearance late yesterday. That Dom was found dead forty feet from Crystal Creek remains as much a mystery as the woman's disappearance.

How are the two connected? Did Dorothy Powell shoot and kill the Mafia operative? Or was someone else there to defend her?

"We know Lorene Perkins was the last person who heard from her," Galena says. "She was told to put two books in the mailbox."

"I read your report regarding Ms. Perkins' testimony," Marilyn recalls. "Do we know the importance of these books to Ms. Powell?"

"No, ma'am." But Galena suspected one of those books was *The Secret Garden*, a children's book that was key to another case.

Marilyn scratches her itchy lip, pondering the detective's answer. "Do we know why Dorothy was alone near Crystal Creek?"

"According to Ms. Perkins, she wanted to say a final goodbye to her deceased husband Arthur, so took a stroll down Crystal Creek."

Marilyn nods. "Nobody went with her."

Galena shakes her head. "As far as we know."

"Dominick was found forty feet from Crystal Creek, shot in the heart by someone. If Ms. Powell didn't shoot him, who did?" Marilyn jerks a breath. "Then leaves no trace of forensic evidence."

Shaking her head, frustrated to the max, Galena shifts her weight from one boot to the other. "Yes, Ma'am. *Nada*."

Frustrated, Marilyn slams a fist on the desk. "I swear, Detective, if you call me ma'am one more time I'm going to scream."

Galena recognizes the captain has reached a tipping point to her patience after the coroner found nothing conclusive to report.

"Sorry, uh, Captain Colbert," she reluctantly answers.

Marilyn points to the door. "Go get me more information."

Galena nods. "I'm interviewing everyone close to Ms. Powell."

"Carry on. I'll get things going at my end."

"Yes, uh, of course."

Galena exits the office, relieved to have that conversation behind her. As she steps off the elevator, the officer manning the front desk downstairs makes a pass at her. She gives James the same speech she gave all the others guys in town who want to date her.

"I'll get back to you about coffee later in the week."

But she never does. No time for personal relationships.

* * *

Captain Colbert stands in front of twenty officers under her command in the conference room on the lower level of the concrete-block building that sits on a half-acre plot of land in the business district of Columbia, Tennessee. Fourteen seasoned male and female police officers fill three rows of chairs, alert and awaiting special instructions. Marilyn stands tall at the lectern and clears her throat.

"You have been chosen as a special task force designated to locate a missing person, Dorothy Jean Powell. Eighty-three years old, she's the widow of Arthur Clark Powell who was murdered three years ago this October. Locate and bring her home, dead or alive."

Officer Peter Quinn rises to his feet.

"I was the first officer to respond to the 9-1-1 call at 404 Highway 7 yesterday at 5:57 p.m." He clears his throat. "Me and my partner, Henry—sittin' beside me." He glances down. "We found the murdered victim lying in the grassy field near Crystal Creek."

Marilyn raises a hand to halt his speech.

"Is there a point you wish to make, Officer Quinn?"

This meeting was not to hash out specific details.

"No, just saying." Peter sits down. Several officers chuckle.

"Okay then, here is how we will proceed." The screen behind Marilyn ignites with a geographical photo of the 200-acre farm once owned by Ms. Powell, but sold to Ellie Simpson this past February.

"Here is our territory." Marilyn taps her pointer on the screen. "I want every exit point leaving this farm walked over. Every field examined. Every physical structure searched. If you find even a loose hair, or bobby pin, I want it processed as evidence. Are we clear?"

No words. Only nods. Tensions are high.

"Office Joellen Jones, you are in charge. Let's get to it, team."

* * *

Ellie Simpson is at Lorene Perkins' house, hoping her presence will have a calming effect. Lorene's been hysterical ever since the black man was found dead not far from Crystal Creek. On sleeping meds since the shooting, she isn't faring well. Graham Perkins and his wife Cynthia are away from the house working today, so Lorene's youngest son Sam, a firefighter, is staying with his mother.

Lorene is presently in her bedroom sleeping off the meds. Sam is seated on the den sofa, his hands unsteady and body twitching.

"I wish I knew how to help Mama," he comments to Ellie.

"She keeps talking about Crawford and how he was murdered by that serial killer," Ellie tells Sam. "She worries she's in danger, too."

"I know." Sam nods. "Dorothy is Mama's best friend. They shared secrets—like soul sisters. I've never seen Mama so upset like this since the day Daddy was found dead near Crystal Creek."

"The creek appears to be cursed," Ellie spouts. "I think it belongs to the Devil." She realizes how ridiculous that sounds.

A noise comes from Lorene's bedroom.

"Should I check on her?" Ellie inquires.

"I will," Sam volunteers and rises to his feet.

He walks the length of the den and enters the hall. A minute later, he quietly opens the master bedroom door. His mama's quiet rasps indicate she is dreaming. He returns to the den.

"Mama's fine. Just a nightmare."

"I wish I knew how to comfort her." Ellie feels helpless.

"We can't. She'll have to work through her feelings by herself." He glares a moment. "I need some fresh air. Let's go out on the back porch." He leads the way with Ellie a few steps behind him.

"Does Lorene blame herself for Dorothy's disappearance?"

"Why should she?" Sam reacts. "Oh. Placing the two books in your mailbox at Dorothy's request." He stares at the plank floor.

"What can I do to assist you?" Ellie asks with sincerity.

Sam shifts his weight from one leather boot to the other. Neighbors have brought in food so he doesn't need a cook. His weary mother will likely sleep for most of the morning.

"Sam? I really want to help you," Ellie insists.

"Stay the day. I need to get to work now. Graham has the early shift at Walgreen's pharmacy and promises to be home by six."

Ellie thinks about her plans for the day. Nothing critical.

"Do you have the time? I'm worried about my mother."

"Of course, I do. No worries. Maybe I can distract her from thinking about Dorothy," Ellies responds. "We'll keep busy."

Sam laughs out loud. "Mama has a mind of her own."

"I'll take her to town for coffee," Ellie suggests.

"Don't go to Coffee Call, Ellie. She's spent too much time with Dorothy there." He recalls the lethal drink Gloria Bolton ingested.

"I'll remind Lorene that Dorothy was kidnapped before and survived," Ellie says. "She's resilient like no one I've ever known."

2

"TOO MUCH PROFANITY?" CIA Thomas Kessler looks down at Dorothy Powell, alias Daphanie Daniels. They are on a private jet enroute to a country in the Middle East since Russia is in the process of invading Ukraine with missiles. He notes her concern.

"Cat got your tongue, Daphanie?"

"I could live with less F's coming out of your mouth," I reply.

He nods. "You have a lot to learn about spying lingo."

"I'd rather not increase my profanity vocabulary." I am still upset he's kidnapped me. "I'm not a spy, send me home."

"Not an option." Mischief resides in his brooding gaze.

"At least you've agreed to explain why you used me as a tool to retrieve the little black book of numbers from the bank in Knoxville, Tennessee. But where does Agent Charlie Darby fit into the picture, and who were you talking to on the phone a few minutes ago?"

Tom drops in a seat next to Dorothy. "Which question do you want me to answer first?" He grasps her cold hand. "Judy, bring our guest a cup of hot coffee—with real caffeine and no sedatives?"

"Cute." Dorothy chuckles. "Who was on the phone?"

"I was talking to the guy on the ground in Pakistan," he replies.

"I thought we were going to Russia."

"Not anymore. The best laid plans sometimes change."

"Don't I know it." I profoundly sigh. Late afternoon, July 4th, I was on my way to Crystal Creek to say my final goodbye to Arthur when havoc struck again. A bullet whizzed past my cheek. My shaky hand wiped away a streak of red blood. Then Tom appeared.

"Look, Daphanie—you need to chill out and go with the flow," he tells me. "Adjust to your new name and get on board with my program, or you'll seriously slip up when it comes time to shine."

I cannot help from clamping my parched lips. My body inadvertently stiffens. "Is that so? I'm not a trained CIA operative."

"Yet, I trust you. Plus, you've read enough spy novels to know when to talk and when less words work to your advantage."

I will soon learn the sting Tom has in mind is complicated and probably dangerous. "Why me? You must have female operatives."

"I do." He grins and I hate him. "But I want you."

"What if I disagree with your agenda?"

"Don't. Trust me. I promise everything will work out just fine."

Fine? I want to bawl, but I stiffen in my comfortable seat, buckled in, so I won't fall into the aisle every time the private jet hits a wind bump. Trusting Tom is difficult since he kidnapped me.

"What are you thinking, Daphanie?"

I look at him hard. "That's not my name."

"It is now. Be honest with me."

"Okay. I have my doubts about your mental stability."

Tom squeezes my hand. I despise that he can get to me so easily. I love him and he knows it. Our ages are too far apart. A sexual relationship would complicate my life and make his worse. Yet, every time I am around him, the world comes more alive and appealing. Should I resist such a high calling to help America?

Or am I just pleasing Tom?

"I'm not crazy." He becomes serious. "Nobody else can do what I have in mind better, trust me. Otherwise, I would never have had your back when Dominick Karensky came calling on the 4th."

Our coffee arrives, defining the moment, a truth I don't like.

"Did you add cream and sugar to mine?" I ask Judy.

"Just as prescribed." She trots off to the back of the plane.

"You told her how I like my coffee?" Tom is full of surprises.

He glances over, stretches out his long lanky legs. "It was all in the dossier. Everything about you from birth to eighty-two."

I glare at him in disbelief. "Seriously? You have to remind me of my age? Actually, I'm eighty-three, you cad!" I slam him in the chest.

"Ouch." He yanks his head to one side. "Just being honest. . ."

"Okay, while we're being honest, was your earlier declaration of love genuine? Do you really care about my wellbeing and health?"

"I meant every word of it. Drink your coffee, Daphanie."

I grab a sip, uninterested in coffee.

"How can I trust you now that I know you would've let that Russian criminal Dom kill me if you didn't have future plans for our liaison—whatever that is!" I explode. "I'm only a pawn on the CIA chessboard." The hurt in me mounts but I deny a flood of tears.

Tom's expression visibly mellows as his features soften and he places a hand under my quivering chin. "You know I have a soft spot for you, Blondie." He leans too close to my face for comfort.

Is he going to kiss me?"

I push him away. "Only because I resemble your dead wife. You are seriously a sick person, Thomas Kessler."

He leans back, shrugging. "I have a job to do."

Then looks at me with those dark brooding eyes.

"Look, Daphanie. I've been at this spy thing for forty years," he tells me. "I know what I'm doing. Do what I say and you'll be fine."

As he closes the gap between our lips, I slap him hard.

* * *

Folks in Middle Tennessee who know Dorothy Powell are worried about her. Especially her daughter Claire Burkes.

"You need to stop crying," Husband Ted tells her. "The police will find your mother." It's not the time to leave her for his mistress.

Claire swipes the tears from her red cheeks. "But will they find her alive?" She worries the Russian Mafia has kidnapped her.

Ted pulls Claire from the sofa and hugs her. "Look, honey, I talked to Detective Chico. Whoever ran off with your mother killed the black man that was stalking her. I don't think he'll hurt her."

"You're sure it's a man?"

"No, I just assume."

"What about Zoey Jackson's suicide? Did the Columbia Police Department ever find out what really happened to her?" Claire asks.

Ted lets her go and shakes his head. "Quit inventing reasons to worry, Claire. Let's just go out and enjoy a rare steak at a restaurant."

She nods. "Okay, I sure do not feel like cooking tonight."

Claire's cell phone rings.

"Yes?"

"Ms. Burke, this is Detective Chico."

"Did you find my mother?" Claire asks.

"We found evidence that she boarded a private jet at a private airport south of Franklin. No flight information was made available."

"You can't find out where the plane was going?"

"That will take a court order, Ms. Burke. We'll find out, but not today. Have a good evening. We're on it," Galena says.

Claire ends the call.

"Who was that, honey?" Ted calls out from the den.

"Detective Chico. She has a lead on Mama."

Claire stands motionless, in deep thought.

"That's good," Ted says. "I told you the police will find her."

She hasn't moved a muscle. Worrisome.

"Are you ready to leave for the restaurant?" Ted asks.

"No, I still have to get dressed and call the kids. They will want an update on GG." Claire thinks particularly of June, how attached she's become to her great-grandmother. "I'll hurry."

Ted trails Claire down the hall and into their bedroom.

"Honey, I'm so sorry this has happened. You've had enough trauma with your mother recently. This is but another bump."

"It's more than a bump, Ted. This situation is serious. You know how difficult Mama has become since Daddy's death."

Unpredictable, Ted thinks but instead says, "We'll get through this difficult junction together, honey. Somehow. I promise."

Claire faces Ted, her pink cheeks wet with tears.

"Thank you for being so supportive, Ted."

"I'm doing my best." He releases a prolonged sigh.

3

Thursday, July 6

"WHO'S HERE IN PAKISTAN?" I ask Tom as we sit under the striped tent of a street-side restaurant located in the Pakistani Express Market—better known by Americans as a Farmer's Market. The metropolitan city of Karachi is Pakistan's capital in the Province of Sindh. Claire would be so proud of me as a history buff.

"We are," Tom utters, shooting me a steely look.

"Cute." I sigh. He's full of humor—which reminds me that I am not, especially since a bullet grazed my cheek three days ago as I attempted to say goodbye to Arthur on the banks of Crystal Creek.

"Don't go to any place dark," Tom tells me.

I am already there. True, we are here, but that does not make me feel warm and fuzzy. Dozens of Muslims wearing their foreign garb trek past us on their way to God-Knows-Where. Never once do they glance our way. We are pariahs, American ants that need squashing beneath their dusty sandaled feet. Filthy white infidels.

I lock my gaze on Tom. He is beautiful. Handsome, intelligent, wily, interesting, scary, and far too young for me to love.

"I still wonder why we are here." I take a sip of my coffee, so strong it looks like ink and attacks my stomach as it trickles down.

He leans forward, a silly little smile at the corner of one lip. "I like you, Dorothy. I promise to keep you safe. Don't be concerned."

I sit back, pushing my ceramic cup away from me on the table.

"Of course not, Thomas! I am thousands of miles away from my home, in a country that hates me because I am white, and with a man who kidnapped me. What's there to be concerned about?"

I look away, tears threatening, then shrug like it doesn't matter.

He chuckles. "You're fun, Dorothy. But you know that."

If only I had a snapshot of my expression. I can tell by Tom's that he knows I despise his comment. Nothing about this is fun.

"So, my GGD tells me." I refer to June then think of Claire who must be worried sick about me. Lorene has probably already had a nervous breakdown. She wonders who is coming after her next.

A puzzle is squirreled away in Tom's handsome face.

"Oh, GGD stands for my great-granddaughter," I decipher. "Don't be concerned. You will never understand a five-year old."

He laughs. "I saw you Googling Pakistan."

I drag my cup closer and sip the thick brew.

"I know something about this country. Its history is stormy. After World War II, Great Britain gave up its control over it."

"Then you know that Muslims are ruling and very religious. They take their five tenants grounded in Muhammad quite seriously."

I point to the silk scarf covering my head. "I'm obedient. No need for them to chop off my head. When can I go home, Tom?"

"Not until we do what we've come for," he replies, signaling for the barista to bring us our tab. He pays in American cash.

The waitress trots off smiling; two dark holes in the front of her mouth gape like caves. She seriously needs the attention of a dentist.

"I think the server likes you."

"I gave her twenty dollars for two coffees. What's not to like?"

"Which reminds me, what did you do with my billfold with all my American credentials inside?" I have a new identity, but isn't it for a short period of time? One day I will need Dorothy Jean Powell back. I don't want my tombstone to read DAPHANIE DANIELS.

"Let me take care of the details while you follow my directions."

"I thought our sting was to be carried out in Russia."

"Let's go back to the hotel and I'll go over the details with you."

Finally, I think to myself, I will learn what trouble I've gotten myself into, and why the dadgum little black book is so important.

Back at the Hilton, Tom and I sit opposite at a round table overlooking downtown. I glimpse the horizon of the Arabian Sea a mile away. I've heard Quaid-e-Azam House Museum is worth a visit.

"What do you want to do today, Daphanie."

"I guess practice being my new self." I give up hope that I might not have to march into a bank and lie about my identity.

"Okay then . . ." he rolls out a large map of Pakistan. "Here are the cities we need to visit before we leave the Middle East."

I look at him, my mouth gaping. "How long is all this going to take?" My shoulders give way and I lean on the table for support.

"As long as it takes." He sits back, rolls the map of Pakistan over to a new page and points to a city map of Karachi. "Here."

I slap his hand. "Here, where? And why?"

"Don't get mean, Daphanie. Our work is important."

"Why?" I quote Psalm 36:1-4. "Sin lurks deep in the hearts of the wicked, forever urging them on to evil deed. They have no fear of God to hold them back. Instead, in their conceit, they think they can hide their evil deeds and not get caught." I stare at him. "I'm the daughter of a Methodist minister. Once, he made me memorize this scripture when I lied to him about where I was after midnight."

"Evil's thirst for violence is never quenched," Tom says. "I read that somewhere—not original but makes a poignant point."

"Okay, at least we agree on something," I say. "We want to stop the bad guys and make them pay. We want to prove that Agent Charlie works for the SVR. I get that. Why me, Tom? I am nothing."

Tom shakes his head, grinning. "No, Daphanie, you're definitely *not* nothing. You are clever, determined, and focused. I love you."

I want to say *I love you, too*, but I don't. It isn't proper. Something bad might happen. I might crawl in that big bed and let Tom explore my possibilities. "Tell me what to do," I say instead.

* * *

Back in Columbia, Tennessee, Captain Marilyn Colbert shuts the door to Detective Chico's office and leans against it. The whites in her eyes are red from lack of sleep. Her mood is a damp dark.

"Tell me you found evidence that Dorothy Powell still lives."

Galena pushes her ergonomic chair away from the desk, stands up, and rolls her tight shoulders. "Did your team of officers find anything left behind to indicate where Ms. Powell went on July 4th?"

Marilyn drags up a chair and sits down. "Your question does not answer mine." She heaves a breath. "Zip. Just the dead guy."

Galena turns around and pours Marilyn a ceramic mug of black coffee then hands it to her across the desk. "Enjoy. Made fresh."

Marilyn takes a sip. "Starbucks?"

"Dunkin Donuts, my budget is lower than yours."

They both laugh, breaking the tension in the office.

Galena sits back down, says, "I don't think Ms. Powell left the farm by her own volition. But who took her, the good or bad guys?"

"What about Agent Thomas Kessler? Has he been sighted?"

"I have four officers visiting every small airport in Middle Tennessee investigating any night flights on Tuesday," Galena replies.

"You believe Ms. Powell is not in the state," Marilyn concludes.

"I don't think she's even in the country. I had my friend at TBI post her photo on every major federal spy program in existence."

Marilyn nods. "Good. Then I guess we wait for a lead."

Galena nods back as the captain gets up, folds the metal chair, and exits the office. She's no more out of sight before Galena's cell phone rings. "Tell me you have something, Kent."

"A small jet departed a small, privately-owned airport south of Franklin," he reports. "The manager said the pilot filed no flight plan." He pauses. "Isn't that illegal, using U.S. airspace?"

"Damn straight it's illegal!" Galena replies.

"I don't know how else I can help out," Kent admits.

"You can't. I'll let Captain Colbert know so she can call in her fourteen agents on a wild-goose chase. Thanks for the quick update."

Galena ends the call and phones Captain Colbert's cell phone.

* * *

Claire is still in a tether. "What am I going to tell our children?" She glares at husband as he enters their home in Brentwood. A truck might have run over him considering the bruises on his left cheek.

"Did someone hit you. Ted?"

"No, no! I ran into the corner of an open cabinet in the kitchen at my office." He sets his briefcase on the floor and pecks Claire on the cheek. "I gather you didn't have the best of days either."

He's not about to confess he broke off with his lover and she walloped him with a frying pan. Considering Natalie is pregnant, he can't blame her. But neither can he leave Claire under these unusual circumstances. Natalie would just have to get an abortion.

"Detective Chico phoned a few minutes ago. The police believe Mama was flown out of Tennessee Tuesday evening in a private jet," Claire reveals. "I want you to hire a PI to track down my mother."

Ted collapses in a barstool in the kitchen and rests his forearms on the bar. "Where was the jet headed?" His face hurt like hell.

"The pilot didn't file a flight plan."

"That's not legal. The feds will be all over this," Ted says.

"It was a privately-owned airport," Claire reveals.

Ted grasps his achy head. "I need to go to bed, Claire. Can we talk about this tomorrow? I've had a dreadful day, too."

Claire longingly looks at her husband. She smells beer on his breath. Is he telling the truth? Did he get into a bar fight?

"I'm tired too, honey. Let's hit the sack."

4

Friday, July 7

Back in Pakistan

"**ARE YOU READY TO GO?**" Tom asks Daphanie. From this point on, he will not address her by any other name. Dorothy must get used to her new identity or they will both suffer plenty.

"Do I have a choice?"

Daphanie looks like a million-dollar baby. The stunning business suit she wears belongs to the persona of a wealthy American entrepreneur. Hat and shoes, the outfit costs more than his month's salary. Some expenses are necessary. "We all have choices."

"So, you say. I don't feel right wearing these duds."

Her blue eyes are dull from lack of sleep.

"This outfit is not me, Tom." But privately, I like the new me.

He grins. "You look fantastic, Daphanie. Be happy if nobody associates you with the woman who grew up in Podunk, Tennessee."

He notes the angst in her chilly gaze.

"Sorry, I misspoke," he apologizes.

"Careful, City Slick, don't discount what defenses I might be carrying in this expensive Prada purse." His stare does not restrict my tongue. "Besides, Columbia is bustling and on the verge of growth."

He nods. "Okay, you win this dispute."

"So, what are we waiting for?" I inquire.

"Nothing, unless you want to go over your role in this sting one more time." He waits for my declaration of readiness.

"I know my script, but I'm not happy—just so you know."

He nods. "Sometimes the end justifies the means."

Spy speak, I mentally review what Tom told me last night about the Karachi branch of the Habib Bank of Ag Zurich.

"The financial institution's motto is trust, service, and commitment to customers, always using discretion," I review the information. "I will go inside the bank, present my credentials to the teller, then say I need to close my account and move my funds. I assume the teller will be female, but could be male. That done, I request access to my lockbox," I say. "Easy as eating pie, right?"

"Correct." Tom chuckles. "I will be waiting in our ride outside the bank. If you run into trouble, phone me."

"Do you anticipate a problem?" My heart stutters at the idea.

"No, just saying . . ."

"You said a lot of things last night, Thomas."

He remains silent while I straighten the hem of my Gucci suit jacket as I stand before a floor-length mirror in the Hilton's best suite. I'm wearing a genuine pearl necklace with matching earrings, probably stolen. Tom has spared no expense with his attempt to expose CIA Agent Charlie for his participation in a laundering scheme to hide drug money collected within the borders of the United States. I want him to tell me he's sorry he kidnapped me.

"Bank opens in five minutes, let's head on out," he says.

We exit the Hilton through the foyer and get into a stretch-white limousine Tom rented for the morning. All in the name of justice.

The JS Karachi Group is located on the 6th floor of the Fayal House on Main Shahra-e-Faisal. It takes us fifteen minutes to get there. Tom squeezes my hand before I exit the limousine.

Time to shine or be arrested. Which will it be?

I'm greeted at the branch's door and shown immediately into an office where a dark-skinned Pakistani sits tall at his desk. He sees me and stands to greet me. "Welcome to Karachi, Miss Daniels."

Does he recognize me? That makes no sense. No, the greeter probably gave him my name. Lifting a prayer, I let out a slow breath.

"Thank you for seeing me on such short notice." I sit in the comfortable armchair he points to. "I won't take a lot of your time."

My mind is flirting with what to say next. And it's a good thing I had the lead female part in Arthur's senior-high-school play. As I recall Gerry Bolton was the lead male. He must be missing me, too.

I am with Tom now. *But for how long?*

"What can we do for you today?"

"Mr. Mughal, I need to get inside my lockbox." I hand him the number typed on a piece of paper. "And I'm closing my account."

"Today?"

"Yes." Tom warned me not to add "Sir."

"Account number, please?"

I rattle off the number Tom had me memorize and wait while he checks my balance. He fingers the keys to access his computer.

"Two million, one-hundred fifty-nine rupees?" I nearly scream when he tells me the balance. My poor heart is huffing.

"Yes, did you think you had more?" he inquires.

"No, no, I trust the bank explicitly." It will take a calculator to figure out the total amount of Daphanie's funds in U.S. dollars. Tom had told me that one rupee is equal to $185.32 in U.S. dollars.

"Of course, our motto is trust, service, and commitment." He pauses and glares at his computer. "I see no one has been here physically since 1990 when the account was set up. Yet, um, deposits have been transferred monthly from a bank in District of Columbia."

"The U.S. Correct." What do I know about laundering drug money? I want to get this job done and go. My family misses me.

"Do you want to access your lockbox before I transfer funds?"

"Yes." I can think of no better word of compliance.

But privately I wonder if I should phone Tom and tell him the amount of Daphanie's account. He notices my hesitancy.

"Is there a problem?" Mr. Mughal inquires.

"No. Is there a restroom nearby?" My bladder doesn't call, but I need to be alone to phone Tom. I wait for instructions.

The marble floor echoes my heels clicking on its hard surface.

A female wearing a hijab, or dress, with a khimar, or head scarf, greets me at the restroom door with a small roll of tissue.

I'd read about the culture last night online and learned ninety-percent of Pakistani residents practice Islam. I hand the woman an American dollar as a tip in exchange for the wipes.

She smiles at me, grateful with a slight head bow. Women here are subservient. It's a way of life I never learned.

The closet has a door so I step inside and close it, deciding I might as well wee-wee while here. I am alone so I make the call.

"Are you all right, Daphanie?"

"Yes, Tom, I'm fine. Things are going well. I just need to see what's inside the lockbox and transfer the funds to our new account." Then I tell him what Mr. Mughal told me.

"Good. Carry on." He ends the call.

The manager is waiting in his office with the bank's key to the lockbox. I pilfer through my purse and look up at him distressed.

"I must have misplaced my key." I look at him. "I had it yesterday. Will that be a problem? Considering the amount of my funds?" I need to convince him to let me see inside the box.

He doesn't look pleased. "I need to make a call."

"Of course, I'd expect no less."

I am left alone as he steps across the hall.

He is back in ten minutes.

"We'll waive the second key, considering the circumstances."

That's the second indication I am recognized. It makes no sense. I have never been in Pakistan. I haven't even been to Europe.

"Oh, thank you, Mr. Mughal. As you see I am growing older, and wish to distribute my wealth among my many younger relatives."

"I understand. Shall we step down the hall to the vault?"

I trail him, feeling I might actually succeed at this sting. I'm on the CIA payroll, but if Tom and I keep Daphanie's money, we could buy a remote island in the South Seas. And live happy-ever-after?

What about my family? I need to go home.

Mr. Mughal sets the metal box on a table and leaves the room. I flip open the lid to the lockbox and glare at dozens of packs of Bearer Bonds. I feel faint. The room swirls around me. How can I carry so many bonds? My purse is not that big. I open the door.

Mr. Mughal looks at me for direction.

"Come in, please," I tell him.

The stacks of thirty Bearer Bonds sit on the table.

"Do you want me to put those in a bag for you?"

My tongue won't work. I am nauseous. And scared.

"Miss Daniels, are you ill? Shall I call a physician?"

"Give me a minute. I'm hypoglycemic." It's my first thought to explain my dizziness. Soon, I am breathing normally.

He retrieves a nylon bag from a slender closet and loads it with *my* bonds. I own them now since whoever has them in their possession can cash them. I never saw myself as a criminal.

Until now.

I am tempted to march out the backdoor of the bank with my bonds, hail down a city cab, and go straight to the airport with this mega-bag of Bearer Bonds. But a good Methodist will not do that.

We are back in Mr. Mughal's office. The transfer of funds to the new account to a bank in Australia goes off without a hitch. A few key-clicks on the Apple Computer and the money belongs to me.

Or Tom. I suspect he'll give it to the CIA.

Of course, we can't keep it.

Dare we?

5

WE ARE BACK AT the Hilton and packing our bags. "You didn't tell me where we are going next?" I gather my toothbrush and toiletries into a floral bag. "And you never said you were proud of me."

I look at him, sure that my disappointment shows.

"I'd rather show you."

Tom walks my way, that silly grin on his face.

"What?" I worry about what comes next.

Before I know it, I am in his arms and we are kissing. Not pecking like Ted and Claire. More like Humphrey Boggart and Greta Garbo. Our mouths are lip-locked, and damn if I don't want to let go and respond. But somebody has to have good judgment.

I shove Tom away. "Nice, but I'm not for sale."

He appears wounded. "I would never—"

"What? Use me to get to the money? Kidnap me and forbid me to call my daughter? Wine and dine me, have sex with me, then dump me?" I'm on a roll. "I guess not. You're the perfect gentleman."

He slumps to the bar and pours himself a glass of chardonnay.

"It's too early to start drinking," I say.

"It's five o'clock somewhere." He gulps down several ounces.

"Okay, I'm sorry if I hurt your feelings. But you are not being entirely honest with me, Tom. There can be no intimacy between us without trust. Why did I feel like people at the bank knew me?"

He straightens his spine and rolls around on the barstool.

"What do you mean?"

"Mr. Mughal barely hesitated in providing a second key to the lockbox," I inform him. "He acts like he knows Daphanie Daniels."

I am troubled by all the mystery that shrouds me.

Tom takes my hand and quietly leads me to the sofa. "Are you sure you want all the details? Knowledge can be dangerous."

I sit down, nod, and wait for Armageddon to strike.

"Look, you are not going to like what I tell you."

"I already don't like what you've told me."

He places his hands on his knees. "You already know my wife was murdered twenty-two years ago by Mark Hagen. But what you don't know is that she was undercover for the Russian Mafia. I was targeted as a CIA agent. She was assigned to get information out of me and pass it on to her drug bosses. But we fell in love."

I am listening, but not believing my ears.

"So, she turned on them. And we married."

I am so stunned I'm speechless.

"Then she told me about the foreign bank accounts she had set up in the early nineties for the Russian Mafia peddling drugs on American streets. You were chosen to help the CIA since you resemble Daphanie Daniels. That's who my wife was before she was Angela Kessler. Then she was murdered. Then my life ended."

I take in a huge breath. "So, it was not a coincidence you flirted with me after you moved to Columbia to run the Senior Citizen Center. You used me. How long did it take the CIA to find me?"

"When Arthur was murdered, an asset recognized you at his funeral and called me. I'm sorry. I didn't know you then like I know you now." There were genuine tears in his eyes. "I'm so sorry."

I do not know how to react. I have murder in my heart.

Jesus, forgive me.

But if I had a gun, there wouldn't be enough bullets to put Thomas Kessler permanently in his grave. I'd make sure there was no tombstone to honor him. I would throw his body in the ocean and disappear somewhere to live the rest of my life on the Bearer Bonds. But I cannot, because I love him. So, I weep.

✞ ✞ ✞

Back in Columbia, it's a normal Friday afternoon at the Senior Citizen Center. Lorene Perkins sits at a table for four holding thirteen Canasta cards in her shaky hands. She lays down a red three and draws a third card from the stack. Then discards one.

"Do they know where Dorothy went?" Lizzy Hinson asks as she draws two cards and studies her hand for a discard.

"No, but she might not even be in America," Lorene replies.

"I always knew trouble would get her," Jane Murphy—the table's good Presbyterian—remarks. "She's probably dead."

"That's a terrible thing to say!" Beverly Trenton exclaims.

"I agree," Lorene says. Beverly is in the same Sunday School class as Dorothy at the First Methodist Church. She's nice.

Lizzy discards an eight. Beverly is her partner, so Jane draws two cards, lays down a red three, then draws a third card. She can meld.

Four eights and three aces. Nice.

"Did they ever arrest anyone for Gloria Bolton's death?" Jane inquires. "The article in the paper stated Zoey Jackson's death has not yet been proven as a murder." She discards a black four.

"Do we have to talk about death?" Lorene pipes. "I miss my best friend, so I just want to play cards and forget about the terrible things happening in Columbia." She takes her turn playing.

* * *

Dorothy/Daphanie sits next to Clint/Thomas in a priority section of the Emirates airplane headed for Dubai. The commuter jet is about to land. All he can see out of the narrow window is sand and tall modern buildings. They are not sharing thoughts.

For the best, Tom thinks. He has a plan. He hopes Dorothy will be onboard when he lays it out in plain terms. If not, he can't just send her home. She knows too much. Tom looks at her.

The unhappy camper is peeved as the jet sets down at the airport. She stares out the window—despondent. Not a good sign.

"Ready to deboard?" He nudges her with a hand.

She quickly jerks around in her seat to face him.

"What choice do I have?"

He chuckles. "None, unless you want to fly to Egypt."

I don't comment as the plane creeps to the gate at the International Dubai Airport. I have briefly slept, restless dreams my constant companion. Seeing Tom's alertness, I worry more.

We grab our luggage from the overhead bin and thread our way through the tunnel to the airport proper. It's crowded with Muslims.

"Are we safe here?" I implore him as my tongue loosens.

He grasps my hand as we trudge toward BAGGAGE. I have a whole new expensive wardrobe to drag around the planet with us. Tom has only one bag, a no-nonsense traveler with hidden mysteries in that kooky brain of his. I have been used by both Tom and the

CIA, but I refuse to allow him to abuse my heart any further. I must rein in my emotions and alert to anything that appears misleading.

"You're not saying much, MD."

My Dorothy. "Cute, Tom."

"Come on, something is brewing in that kooky brain."

He makes me laugh. "I don't have anything to say of value." I gaze at him as we watch the revolving stage with baggage circle around with my overstuffed suitcase. He scrubs one eye with a fist.

He's tired, too, just not complaining like I am.

"Just so you know, I care about your opinion," he says.

"I've pretty much said it all." I sigh since I think there is more about what's going around us that he is purposely not sharing. But I won't confront him while we are exiting the airport.

"I'm sure you will have questions later," he continues.

"As a matter of fact, where are we staying tonight?" I trail him off the tram and we exit the terminal proper together. The air feels cool though the temperature must be in the nineties. Low humidity.

"The Holiday Inn," he replies, waving down a city taxi.

"I thought we'd at least stay somewhere exotic—considering we are wealthy now." He carries the Bearer Bonds in a leather bag strung from one shoulder while rolling the small bag containing his clothes.

I am, on the other hand, saddled with dragging my heavy suitcase riding on wheels. "Why did you choose the Holiday Inn?"

"For $58 a night, we can get a room with two doubles," he says.

I watch as the cabbie places our luggage in the trunk of the taxi and do not trust doubles to keep us apart in a hotel room.

Tom places the shoulder bag with the Bearer Bonds between us on the backseat like a Mama Turkey guarding her young chick from a hawk or coyote. He gives the Muslim driver the hotel address.

The first thing I notice in Dubai is the tall building that juts up into the sky like a pointed arrow. "What's that thing?" I query Tom.

"Buji Jumara," he replies. "The tallest skyscraper in the world."

The Muslim passes a pamphlet over the front seat with a floorplan of the Buji. There are upscale retail stores for shopping, restaurants with exotic names, business offices on the higher floors, and even residential spaces. I note that the building connects to the Dubai Mall. A popular site we need to see, according to the cabbie.

I am nearly dizzy over what I've missed most of my life. As we drive through the city proper, Tom points out places of interest that we might want to visit while staying over a long weekend. Islamic banks aren't open on Sundays, and most are closed on Mondays.

We exit the cab at the portico of the Holiday Inn, which is located next to the Dubai Festival City Mall. It's an IHG hotel—whatever that is. I don't ask since my knowing isn't worth a bologna sandwich—which I despise but Arthur absolutely salivated over.

Tom retrieves the keycard for our room on the ninth floor.

I think it is too high up for us to escape a fire. I recall that Tom had a rope in his suitcase. I don't think it is for fires. I think it for me if I decide to give him trouble. I'm all in, God help me.

That also might mean jailtime.

* * *

Columbia, Tennessee is usually a quiet city, but today the police force is troubled. "Are we getting anywhere with locating Dorothy Powell?" Captain Colbert asks Detective Chico over her phone.

"Nada," Galena replies. "Not one ping from Dorothy's cell phone. It's evident she's pitched it, or her abductor has."

"We seem to have exhausted our resources in finding her," Marilyn admits. "I think we have to pause until we get a break."

"Like, she finds a way to call her daughter," Galena concludes.

"Yes. Our best hope to locate her."

"And if she doesn't?"

"We assume she is dead."

6

Saturday, July 8

THROUGH THE PICTURE window of our hotel room, I see a clear, sunny day dawning in Dubai. July temps can reach into the hundreds. The sunset last night was spectacular in a desert setting. And Tom was unusually quiet before we parted ways. In the end, he changed our room accommodation with doubles to an adjoining suite.

I refused to sleep in the same bedroom with him. Call me prudish. I am a Methodist. And I'm sticking to my principles.

I'm up early perusing the pamphlets the Muslim cabbie gave us on our ride over to the Holiday Inn yesterday. A noise comes from the adjoining bedroom. Then the turn of a lock, and the door opens.

"Well, look who's up?" Tom tramps barefoot into my room.

I glance up, but do not comment.

"You look nice," he says. I am wearing a silk robe he bought me yesterday. "Did you sleep well?" He heads for the coffeemaker.

After pouring himself a mug of straight-up black java, he limps over to the sofa and casually drops down beside me.

"Thanks for making the coffee."

"I wanted some, too." I fold the pamphlet then place it on the glass-top coffee table. "I slept amazingly well, considering. . ."

A question is on his face.

"I know, you wonder why, *considering* my attitude last night."

"Are you feeling better about our arrangement?" he inquires.

"No, I prayed to God that He would get me out of this mess."

Tom chuckles. "And that makes you feel better, safer?"

I ogle him. "Of course, I trust God with my life."

He shakes his head. "I never thought God did me any favors."

"How often do you read your Bible and pray?"

"Seldom," he says. "Never is more truthful."

I laugh. "Finally, some honesty. There might actually be hope for you," I add. "I know you've sinned. But Jesus forgives."

"So, my mother once told me."

Tom has never talked about his parents. This is a new venue I can explore to learn more about what drives him to CIA nonsense.

"My parents were Missouri farmers," he says, sipping on his black coffee, his chin jutted out as he recalls some of his childhood.

"Did they bootleg? Is that why you chose federal work?"

"No, they were ordinary folks," he tells me, setting his mug on the coffee table and grasping my hand. "They loved each other very much." He shakes his head. "Then God took them from me."

"How?" I am genuinely interested in his past.

"Car accident. I was eleven and my sister was four."

I am alarmed that Tom blames God for accidents.

"I didn't know you had a sister." All this is new information.

"Jeannie. I never see her. Better that way."

"To keep her safe." I nod my head. "God is love. He's good."

"You don't think it was God's fault my parents died?" Tom glares at me. "I prayed they would survive and they didn't."

"We don't always get what we pray for," I say.

"He could've done better. We were raised by a nasty aunt."

I don't know how to respond. God has disappointed Tom. He's chosen to cut his only sister out of his life, but hasn't done much to reach out to Jesus for help or forgiveness. He's admitted he doesn't read his Bible. He doesn't go to church. Will he ever pray again?

Where does that leave me? I'm travelling with an infidel. Surrounded by millions of Muslims who worship Muhammad instead of Jesus. Even if I escape from Tom, I wouldn't know what to do.

"Ah—enough about me." He walks over to the counter and picks up the hotel phone. "What do you want for breakfast?"

I shrug. "We could take a walk and find a café."

"Lovely idea, I'll get dressed."

Our suite is first class. He paid more to please me. Tom respects me, though I wonder why. Perhaps it is only a game to get me to cooperate, which has worked. I misrepresented myself in Pakistan and moved millions of drug dollars to a new account in Australia.

Is Jesus going to forgive me for that?

Thirty minutes later, we are walking down the sidewalk in the heart of Dubai. It's Sunday so mosques are full of weekday workers honoring their faith. We see few people roaming the streets this early in the morning. I wonder if a Christian church exists in this modern city. The café we choose is overflowing with international guests.

I don't see headwraps on any of the women. It's an American café. On the sign outside it reads DUNKIN DONUTS.

Imagine, in Dubai!

Tom orders two ham croissants and two cappuccinos for us as I snag a table for two and drop in a chair to rest my weary feet.

Prada shoes win no contest against my old tennis shoes.

I watch Tom standing in line. He's so handsome. I love his thick graying hair. Arthur had none. I cannot let myself be distracted by teenage impulses. I need a plan to contact Claire. She must be crazy with worry. I've been gone five days. But how? Think, Dorothy.

Tom is back at our table within fifteen minutes. We eat, don't talk—can't for all the noisy conversations. Young children are everywhere screaming. Little pistols firing off for the morning. Parents looking weary and probably sorry they brought their brood on the vacation. We could be in a Nashville fast-food restaurant.

"Tom—I have a problem," I tell him with a flash of inspiration.

He tosses our paper products in a trash bin as we exit Dunkin.

"What kind of problem—did you eat too much breakfast?"

I rub my jaw. "I need to see a dentist. My tooth hurts."

As we walk back the way we came, he thinks about my request.

"I know, it's an inconvenient time, but if I ignore my toothache, it might abscess," I explain. "I'll be no good to you on Tuesday when we visit a bank to move funds." We keep walking. I keep thinking.

He shakes his head. "I don't know if we can find a dental office open today." We walk another block to the Holiday Inn.

"We can ask the concierge at the front desk," I suggest.

We enter the vaulted atrium and approach the desk hosting the concierge. A long train of pamphlets are displayed in plastic trays.

"Excuse me, Miss?" I take control of the expedition.

"How may I help you?" the beautiful Arab responds.

She is a young woman, maybe in her late thirties. Her dark eyes are huge and illusive. She is slender and does not wear traditional

Muslim garb, rather chose to wear a tailored suit with a white blouse. I can't see her feet, but I suspect they are clad in modern-day sandals.

"I need to see a dentist. Is there an emergency clinic nearby?"

She pilfers through her cell phone looking for an address with phone number for a local dental clinic. I wait, toes crossed as she writes down the information on a piece of paper and hands it to me.

"Great! Thank you." I turn around and see Tom is not there.

He's across the corridor using a payphone to make a call. Am I in trouble? Have I made a mistake? Who is he talking to?

"May I ask who you just called?" We are on the elevator going up to the tenth floor. It moves fast. My stomach doesn't.

"A friend—nothing to worry about." He shrugs as the elevator doors swish open and deliver us upon multi-colored plaid carpet.

"I get it—a need-to-know thing." I am not happy with the call.

Our hotel suite has been cleaned. Kudos for the maid.

Tom tosses a set of keys with his billfold on the bar and stares at me. I wait for enlightenment. I wish he'd just spit it out.

"Can you wait until after Tuesday to see a dentist?"

"No, I am in pain, Tom."

Stand your ground, girl.

"Okay. I'll call for an appointment."

"Thank you." I smile sweetly at my abductor.

Chalk that win up for my side!

* * *

It's late Saturday in Tennessee when Claire and Ted are seated in the den at their home in Brentwood. They'd spent the day at the Nashville Zoo—not her idea of a great time, but Ted had promised to attend church tomorrow with the rest of the family.

It is important to Claire that everyone in her family worship Jesus together on Sundays. For months, Ted has stayed home and worked. But now, he realizes how much she misses her mother.

The hour grows late, toward 10 p.m.

"Did you hear anything new from Detective Chico yesterday?" Ted bounces June on his knee. She's giggling and poking his nose.

"Stop it, June. You'll hurt your granddad," Claire admonishes.

Ted sets June on the floor and grasps Claire's hand. "I'm not breakable, honey. And I love when June spends the night with us."

Helen had Billy's Tee-Ball buddies tonight—a slumber party in a tent erected in their backyard. "Are you going over to see the boys?"

"Yeah, around midnight, to relieve the weary parents," Ted replies. "I'll give June a bath first and put her to bed for you."

Claire is surprised. "Really? How thoughtful."

"I've been working too hard lately and missed out on family activities," Ted admits as he grabs his knees and rises from the sofa.

"June!" Claire snags the five-year-old and looks her in the eyes. "No splashing water on the bathroom floor. Promise?"

June nods, a finger stuck between her plump lips. "GG?"

"She's on a vacation," Claire replies. They haven't told her or Billy their great-grandmother is missing—no abducted.

"Having fun," Ted adds, glancing at Claire.

June shrugs. "I wish I could have some fun."

Ted laughs and picks June up. "Let's go splash water on YGM's floor. She'll have to mop it up then. Won't that be fun?"

"Theodore!" Claire exclaims.

He waves her off.

"Have it your way, but I'm heading to bed."

"Don't go to sleep; I might have a few surprises up my sleeve."

Won't that be something? Claire smiles then tromps down the hall.

7

Monday, July 10

IT WAS NOONTIME IN Dubai by the time Tom and I had dressed and made plans for our day. I'd finally convinced him that seeing a dentist about my achy jaw could not wait. An abscess is unacceptable.

He'd called the number the Holiday Inn concierge gave us earlier this morning. I have set my own plan in motion. While he waits in the outer office, I am seated in the reclining dental chair with the female assistant fussing over me. My mouth is prized open with X-ray equipment as she takes several pictures. I am miserable.

Dr. Karoum returns to the office ten minutes later to examine the films then explores the inner workings of my mouth with his metal instrument. "I don't see a problem, Miss Daniels," he reports.

"Then why does my mouth hurt?" I have a plan but opportunity has not yet knocked. I need to play out this fake scene.

"Could be a nerve problem—shall I make you an appointment with a neurologist?" He twists his thick Arab lips, those black eyes on me like a spider about to leap. "I could set it up right now."

I'm thinking of how I can lure him out of the room so I can borrow the assistant's cell phone. "Is there a consultation cost?"

"Yes." He quotes an approximate price in a currency I'm unfamiliar with, so I say, "May I borrow a phone and check with my insurance company?" It's the only way I can contact Claire incognito without Tom finding out. I am handed a cellphone.

"What happened to yours?" Raji the assistant asks.

"I misplaced it, sorry."

They wait for me to make my call.

"If you don't mind, I'd rather do this alone," I tell them.

"Sure." They exit the examination room and shut the door.

Finally. I punch in Claire's cell number and pray she will answer. I know in Tennessee it's much earlier in the day—ten hours maybe?

No answer. She's probably still sleeping.

I wait and wait and wait . . . then pray and pray and pray.

The call goes to voicemail. *Double DD!* I curse to myself.

I leave a message that I'm okay and working on a plan to come home soon. I do not mention Tom since I don't want to get him in trouble. The CIA might pick up his name over the airways.

I place the phone on my lap and try to relax. The female assistant returns to the room and stands by me.

"Did you make your call to the insurance agent?"

"Yes, I left a message for him to call me back—it will probably be tomorrow sometime," I tell her. "Give me a prescription for some pain pills and I'll get back to you regarding my next appointment."

"We are closed on Mondays," Raja tells me.

"Okay, then Tuesday." By then I'll have my banking duty behind me and Tom and I will be off to Timbuctoo on a new journey.

I return to the outer office with my prescription for pain and Dr. Karoum's card. Tom is half-sitting, snoozing. I clear my throat.

"Huh?" He startles.

"I'm ready to go, Tom," I nearly shout.

He remains sluggish and unresponsive.

"Wake up, Tom!" I shake him. "I'm done with the dentist."

He leaps forward and nearly tumbles to the floor. Poor guy, he's having trouble keeping up with me. A younger guy just can't outpace and older, more experienced gal like myself. Too bad. I recall I once gave a serial killer sleeping pills to escape his clutches. I wonder what too many pain pills will do to Tom. Bad idea, it might kill him.

"Uh, did you get a root canal?" he asks.

"It's not my tooth causing the pain."

We walk out the door, down the hall, and descend to the main floor in the elevator. "Then what's causing your jaw pain?" he asks.

"Dr. Karoum thinks I should see a neurologist. It might be Trigeminal Neuralgia," I tell him. I know this from Dr. Google.

"Okay. What do you want to do now?"

"Let's get some lunch; we ate mighty early this morning," I suggest. "I also need to stop by a pharmacy to fill a prescription."

"You really do have a toothache," he says while hailing down a city cab. "We can go to the Buji if you want and find a restaurant."

"Great! The pamphlet said the tallest building in the world has everything anybody could want. And my stomach wants to be fed."

* * *

The Tennessee landscape burns brightly early Monday morning. Claire is up and dressed because her granddaughter June is awake. The little girl has been spoiled by her grandfather and wants him to make her pancakes. Claire sits at the bar drinking her second cup of coffee, watching them. They are so adorable together. June worships Ted, and it's obvious he will pull down strongholds to please her.

She checks her voicemail. A call came in late last night.

Probably spam.

If not, the person calling will leave a voicemail, so she listens.

"Claire, this is your mother. I am well, doing a little traveling. I don't want you to worry about me because I'll be home before you know it." A long silence. "I have to go now." *Click.*

The call ends. Claire is shocked. "Ted?"

"What dear? More coffee?"

"Mama phoned last night."

"Where is she?" He adds syrup to June's stack of pancakes.

"GG called and you didn't tell me?" the little girl spouts.

"She left us a message last night, sweetie," Claire says, her gaze locked on Ted. "Mama's fine—says she'll see us before long."

"And horses fly!" Ted exclaims then curses.

"Honey! June." She blinks twice.

"I know what that word means," June says. "It's okay, MD says that word, too. It's not as bad as some of his other words."

Claire thinks Patrick says much worse—like taking the Lord's name in vain. But she won't point it out to June. "Enough said."

Ted sighs. "We'll talk about what to do about the call later."

"When little ears aren't listening?" June adds, her mouth stuffed with food and OJ. "My goodness, grandparents are complicated."

"You are too smart—"

"For my britches?" June says and laughs.

"Okay, I'm getting dressed for the day." Claire looks at Ted. "What time did you get home from Helen's last night?"

"Around four, when the boys finally passed out."

"Okay, I'm going to take June home as soon as we're both dressed." She pats June on the back. "Finish your breakfast."

* * *

CIA Agent Keleana Knotts—Kelly to her acquaintances—has been tracking the breadcrumbs of their misplaced agent, Thomas Kessler, for a month. She was notified by Director Carlton that a bank transfer was made in Karachi, Pakistan on Friday, July 7.

The manager of the JS Group, a branch of the Habib Bank Ag Zurich, confirmed that Daphanie Daniels closed her bank account and collected the items from her lockbox. There was face recognition and credentials verifying her identity so the bank complied. Although Miss Daniels had only one lockbox key, the manager had provided the second key. Tom must be elated at his sidekick's performance.

Kelly had spoken to her associate, Charlie Darby, about the withdrawal. Since Daphanie Daniels was murdered decades ago, the woman closing the account was not her. He speculated that Dorothy Powell had committed the crime. She was still missing from her hometown. The question remains: was she coerced by Thomas?

* * *

Charlie Darby was in his D.C. office when Kelly phoned. According to her report, no confidential information was given by the bank concerning where the money in Pakistan was transferred. The CIA would eventually find out, but time was not on his side.

Tom was a loose cannon and needed to be stopped. Dorothy Powell had all the bank account numbers recorded in the little black book she removed from the First Federal Bank in Knoxville, Tennessee. With Tom's help, they were absconding the profits that belonged to the Russian drug lords. Charlie's life was on the line.

It was time to contact the big boss in Moscow.

When Director Carlton received Kelly's official report regarding their missing agent, he would be stumped over the ruse. But not Charlie—though he did not tell Drop-Dead-Gorgeous Kelly that.

The best secrets were the ones kept, not shared.

For now, Kelly was told to wait in Karachi.

The CIA had become aware that Dorothy Powell went missing on July 4th in Columbia, Tennessee. The local police had requested her photo be posted on all the international spy programs since the *Missing Persons* had been upgraded to an *Abduction*. Charlie had been assigned to monitoring any international calls that went to Dorothy's daughter, Claire Burkes. Such a call had come in in late Sunday night.

* * *

The streets in Dubai are busy by the time Tom and I are out on the street again after visiting the dental office. I am impressed with the layout of the city located on the Arabian Gulf. The Dubai Creek cuts a path right through the city proper, dividing the business district. Buildings are modern and international currencies flow freely.

If only I had invested in Bitcoin—those early birds are billionaires.

I found that exploring the famous landmarks of Islam's history with the man I love cannot get much better—not that life won't sour at any moment. No one knows when or how Fate will strike and unravel a moment of happiness. I sigh, so content I feel guilty.

I pray Claire got my phone message.

"Are you enjoying sightseeing?" Tom asks, more relaxed than I've seen him all week. He trusts me, his mistake.

"Very much. You've planned well."

He smiles. "I assume that your mouth feels better."

"No pain right now—a puzzle. But I'll take it." I laugh.

"We need to eat an early supper and get back to the hotel. I want you to get a good night's sleep. You have a big day tomorrow."

"Every day is a big day for me." I think of how short life feels.

"Still, I want you alert and ready to shine in the morning."

"I'll do my best." Cooperation will keep me safe for now. "Do you know how much money is in the Islamic Bank of Dubai?"

"I know how much Daphanie deposited in 1990, but the Russians have deposited profits in banks all over the world since then. You'll find out how much when you close all the accounts."

"Are we sending the funds to the same location?"

"God, no."

"Profanity, Tom. I don't put up with it."

"You never said a curse word?"

"My granddaughter June has taught me that capital letters work better—so God does not notice," I tell him and laugh and miss her.

"Funny girl. What kind of food do you want tonight?"

"Let's order from the hotel restaurant. These Prada shoes are killing my feet," I admit. "I appreciate the wardrobe—don't get me wrong. But I'm a country girl and prefer jeans and tennis shoes."

"After you make the bank transfer, I'll take you any place in the world you want to go," Tom says. I don't think home is a choice.

8

Tuesday, July 11

TOM AND I ARE in flight to London, England. I've always wanted to visit European castles. He is keeping his word. I transferred 7.8 billion dollars to a bank in Japan—Tom says they are friendly toward Americans. What about World War II? Not so much then.

"You were great with the bank manager, Daphanie."

"Can I be Dorothy until we land in London?"

"Okay, Dorothy." He hands me his phone with information on famous places to visit in England. "We can go to France, too."

I raise an eyebrow. "You're spoiling me."

"I was thinking we might get married at one of the castles."

I am shocked. I may look like I'm in my late sixties because of Dr. Sharra's magic facelift, but I am fourteen years Tom's senior.

"You're not saying anything."

I feel tears mounting.

"Are you going to cry over a marriage proposal?" he asks.

"I am flattered . . . but marriage is not possible."

"Why not? I love you and you love me."

I want to clobber him. Why did he go and ask me that? He's ruined my international vacation. I turn away and dry my eyes.

"Okay—too soon, I get it."

I am quiet as the weather after a typhoon passes through. My stomach hurts, for real. What would my family think of me if I married a spy? No, a bad spy doing illegal things. But I am, too.

* * *

Claire did not want to phone Detective Chico regarding her mother's phone message. She'd left a voicemail for Galena early Monday but had not heard back. That is unacceptable. She is mad.

She ignores Detective Chico's male secretary and dashes through the office, opens the inner office door and glares at Galena.

"You did not return my call?"

Galena closes her cell phone. "Ms. Burkes."

"Why didn't you return my call?" Claire demands.

"I've been on the phone with the police nearly nonstop since yesterday morning trying to track down your mother," Galena replies.

Claire is too pumped to slow down.

"That's no excuse!" she exclaims. "I'll file a complaint."

Galena stands up and walks over to Claire. "I'm sorry. But I had nothing new to report, and I did not want to disappoint you."

Claire's temp notches down from explosive to angry.

"Forgive me, please."

Gasping for breath, Claire's eyes fill with tears. "Mama says she's okay, but I do not believe her. What if that CIA agent has her?"

"You need to sit down before you faint." Galena unfolds a metal chair and gently lowers her guest into it. "Take slow breaths."

Claire has never had a panic attack, so unable to get her breath is a new revelation. "Thank you. May I have a glass of water."

Galena walks to the door and tells Blake. "Get Mrs. Burkes a bottle of water." She gently pats Claire on the shoulder.

Blake delivers the water and Claire drinks. "Thank you."

"Feeling some better now?" Galena wonders if Dorothy's daughter can handle whatever truth is yet to be revealed.

9

Thursday, July 13

"PARIS, FRANCE? REALLY?" I look at Tom and wonder what other mischief he's cooking up for me. "Another bank?"

"No, I need to do something."

"Something you don't want me to know about," I conclude.

"Just business, honey."

"Don't 'honey' me, CIA Tom. I don't trust you." There! I've said what is on my heart. Will he use me as his pawn then disappear into the vapors? I wish this were a movie I could turn off with a remote.

"A business associate has contacted me," he explains, troubled by my comment, I can tell. He needs me to trust him explicitly.

"Okay, a name?"

"You don't know her. She's young, a CIA agent."

I think about what he's said. "How did *Young* find you?" We'd used burner phones and been careful—except for my phoning Claire on the cellphone I borrowed from the dental assistant. *Rafi*, I recall.

"If you want to go to Paris, I can drop you off at the Louvre and you can shop or go to the theatre. I won't be more than a couple of hours at the most. Then we can fly out of the city." He glares at me.

"Leave Europe for where?" I am dizzy with all the traveling.

And to be honest, my body is aching from sore muscles—not to mention my brain is in overkill. I might have a nervous breakdown if I dwell on all the sins I've committed since Independence Day!

Wow! That even sounds ominous.

"We're taking a commuter flight, if that's okay," he tells me.

"Have you checked out of the hotel?" I inquire.

"An hour ago. We're all set to go to the airport."

We have been in London for only two days. I transferred drug funds from the Bank of London yesterday to a new location. That makes three international crimes I have committed—not including impersonating a former SVR operative for the Russians turned CIA.

How much longer can I play his dangerous game?

"I need to pack first." I want to call Lorene and commiserate over my situation. I wonder if Claire has told her about my call.

Thirty minutes later we are boarding the commuter flight to France. I have never been to Paris, so I'm excited to view the Eiffel Tower with my own eyes. I understand you can ride to the top of it, and I will. That is if the Russians don't find me first and shoot me.

* * *

It is mid-afternoon in Paris. Tom has dropped Dorothy off at the Louvre to tour a few of the city's famous landmarks. He is seated under the striped awning of a streetside café in the heart of the city waiting for Agent Keleana Knotts. She set up the appointment.

Tom spots the female agent from twenty feet away. She is drop-dead gorgeous. He stands to greet her. "Welcome to Paris."

Kelly centers her twinkling turquoise eyes on him.

"This is not a social call. What are you drinking?"

"An expresso strait up—thought I might need it."

She plops her purse on the concrete walk and sits.

"I see you've been having some fun," she comments, no smile, all business, just like the job requires. "I'll have one of those, too."

Tom raises a hand to signal over the waiter. "Bring us two more expressos." His brown gaze captures Kelly. "What's the message?"

She sits back, laughs. "Come home."

"Can't." He downs his first espresso in a thimble-size cup.

"We know you are transferring drug money. Why now?"

"Opportunity knocked."

The waiter returns with two more coffees and Tom pays the tab. Then leans forward. "Do you work for the CIA or Charlie?"

Kelly's expression is priceless.

"Is there a difference?" she asks.

"Damn straight, there is."

"Look . . ." she sips the expresso. "Delicious." Then snaps her long neck to one side. Kelly is six-feet tall, perfect figure, with a flawless olive complexion. She comes from Arab stock, so her hair is jet black. In contrast to turquoise eyes, her beauty is incomparable.

"No, you look," Tom says. "Charlie is dirty, or do you already know that?" The look on her face says she is not surprised.

"What are you doing here, Tom? You're better than this."

He snickers. "Since you've come to fetch me, I'll give you a dose of truth. Then you can argue or walk away—tell the CIA you couldn't find me. That I didn't show up for the meeting."

"What dose of truth?" She tentatively sips on her coffee.

"Charlie is a Russian operative—has been since he turned eighteen. He's been helping the Russian drug cartel deposit money in overseas accounts for decades," Tom explains. "Until recently, he did not know where the funds landed—what banks they are sitting in."

Kelly stares into space, digesting Tom's comments.

"And you do," she utters.

Tom nods, a smile tracing his lips.

"How do you know this?" Kelly shoves her cup away, placing strong hands with manicured nails the color of pink silk on the table.

"Clyde Willems—a snitch. He played Poker with Dorothy Powell's husband on Friday nights. Clyde's gambling habit got him in debt to the Russian drug lords. In too deep to survive, he borrowed money from Arthur Powell and Crawford Perkins to settle his debt."

"Go on." Kelly nurses her coffee.

"After Russia's go-to assassin, Mark Hagen, murdered several people in Columbia, Tennessee, I moved there using an alias to investigate the matter," Tom explains. "He killed my wife."

"I read the official report on her death," Kelly recalls.

"Took place not long after we married in 1991."

"I'm sorry, Tom, that must've been rough."

"I never got over it. Dorothy Powell is the spitting image of Daphanie Daniels." Tom jerks a breath and glances around.

"Who is that?"

"My deceased wife," Tom replies.

"I thought her name was Angela."

"We fell in love. Daphanie changed her name, her life, and her focus when she married me. She became a double-agent."

"And turned on the Russians? Wow, that is new revelation."

"Life is funny like that," Tom comments.

"I came alone," Kelly reveals. "I'm not dirty."

"Jesus, I hope not."

"Your deceased wife. . ." Kelly nods. "Go on."

"Daphanie set up the foreign accounts before we married."

"Okay, so you're using Dorothy to transfer drug-cartel money to new accounts as Daphanie Daniels," Kelly concludes. "Interesting."

"More than interesting," Tom says. "Like a trail of breadcrumbs, I've followed the evidence—without alerting Charlie."

Kelly laughs. "He doesn't miss much."

"Clyde Willems undermined the Russians peddling sex in Nashville, Tennessee, when he gave Arthur Powell a children's book for his birthday. Words were circled in the book. Clyde was a hillbilly, but not dumb. He knew he was in danger."

"So . . ."

"The clues in the book meant nothing to Arthur."

"But later, it did to you," Kelly concludes.

"After a lot of deductions."

"Why not just tell Arthur about the drug operation?"

"Willems was scared. This is all clandestine stuff."

"Then what happened?"

"Let me back up a couple of years. After Willems paid off his gambling debts, the Russians became suspicious. Where did he get the money? Did anybody know about their operations?"

"Spooked, huh?"

"You bet. Don't know how they learned the source of Willem's windfall, but Arthur Powell and Crawford Perkins were murdered."

"Because the Russians thought they knew too much."

"They began eliminating threats against their interests."

"And sent in Mark Hagen to take care of business," Kelly says.

"Both men were scared and took out large insurance policies that would payout to their wives when they died," Tom reveals.

"I read where Dorothy was first accused of Arthur's murder."

"Yeah, but the clues soon led in other directions."

"The police let it go, but you didn't," Kelly huffs.

"No, I had a tiger by the tail and began swinging hard."

"You seduced Dorothy because you had a plan."

"Yep." Tom cringes at his despicable ruse to romance a woman that looked like Daphanie. But love had boomeranged on him.

"So, how did you find the accounts with the Russian's money?"

"I found a bank account number scribbled on a piece of paper in one of Charlie's coat pockets. He must have forgotten it was there."

"An account to which bank?"

"First Federal in Knoxville, Tennessee," Tom replies. "I marked the page numbers in the children's book and sent it to Dorothy as a birthday gift in June. She figured out the city and found the bank."

"What was at the bank?"

"A lockbox. Dorothy retrieved a little black book with all the foreign bank account numbers hosting the Russian Drug Cartel's money—from decades. Millions and millions and millions."

"Wow!" Kelly sits back. "Why not just tell Director Carlton?"

"Is he in on it?" Tom glares at Kelly

"Surely you jest!" Kelly remarks. "He's a straight arrow."

"I thought that about Charlie, too—till I found the account number in his pocket. I want everyone involved, not just Charlie."

Kelly blinks those amazing turquoise eyes. "Now you've placed a target on my back. What am I to do about that? Who can I trust?"

"Me," Tom replies. "And no one else. Work with us."

"You and Dorothy."

"No, me and Daphanie. We've done three transfers. There are another two banks in the wing. I need you to tell Charlie you couldn't find me. Let me take all the money, then we'll confront him."

"Because by then, Charlie will have a target on his back."

"Exactly!" Tom exclaims, wondering what trouble Dorothy is cooking up for him. She's been holding her cards to her chest.

10

I WAS SUPPOSED TO meet Tom back at the hotel thirty minutes ago, but I needed to first make a phone call. The internet connection rings three times before Lorene Perkins answers. "Who is this?"

I pray she won't hang up on me.

"Dorothy?" Lorene's voice is shaky.

I laugh. "The CIA should hire you, friend."

"Where are you?"

"Somewhere they cannot find me. How is life in Columbia? Did Jane Murphy replace me with one of her friends in our Canasta Club?" I am full of questions, but no time to hear answers.

"How is life on the run?" Lorene is no-nonsense in motion.

I briefly describe to her what has happened since I left Ellie's property on July 4th. She promptly gives me a piece of her mind as I listen impatiently like a good friend. But I am on a time schedule. I don't want Tom to know I've called the states again.

"Any other complaints?" Let's get this over with.

"No, just that we love you," Lorene says, running out of steam.

"I'm sorry I've been so much trouble," I tell her. "Please don't tell anyone that I phoned. I have an agenda, trust me."

"You always say that. When are you coming home?"

"I don't know. It depends on how things play out."

"Well, at least you're not dead." Lorene sighs.

Why not tell her the truth?

"Tom asked me to marry him and I'm considering it. We have access to the boatload of drug money. We could buy an island."

"And live happy-ever-after disastrously! That's stupid, Dorothy. You're day-dreaming. Tom is using you. He will dump you instantly for a younger woman. He's so . . . good looking."

"I'm good-lookin' too, Lorene. Did you forget I had a facelift? And I have a new expensive wardrobe. Prada shoes. Gucci purse."

"So, you'd choose prestige and wealth over family and friends?"

I am cut by her remark. "I love Claire. You're my best friend, Lorene, but I need to see this thing through—for Tom's sake."

"I think I should tell Claire you called. She worries about you."

"No, don't, let's keep this between us for now."

"Unfortunately, secrets have a way of surfacing," she says.

Don't I know it?

"Be safe, my friend."

"Ditto." I think of the movie where the heroin died violently.

* * *

I am back at the Parisian Hotel since it is only a ten-minute walk from where I phoned Lorene. The burner I used is in a public trashcan. I have my own key to the hotel room so I let myself in without knocking. Tom steps out of the shower wearing only a hand towel around his loin as I push open the bathroom door.

Goodness! Talk about shocked.

"Sorry," he says.

But he is grinning like the Joker in a Batman movie.

"Shouldn't you put something else on?"

"Oh, yeah." He grabs a bath towel from the rack and scrubs his wet thick gray hair with the hand towel. His gaze never leaves my blushing face. His hair is longer—more like movie stars wear theirs.

I giddily stand there, embarrassed yet desperately in love with a traitor to the United States. It's not that I don't cherish the sweet moments Arthur and I shared as a couple, private moments of extreme pleasure and volatile emotions, but I am beyond tempted to surrender to Tom's charm and give all of myself to his pleasure.

Help me Jesus!

He stands motionless—just staring at me. Like it's my time to say something. Dumbbunny, forget that!

"You're blushing, Dorothy. Want to rethink my marriage proposal?" He corners me against the bathroom door.

Lordy mercy! I am putty in his hands.

We hear the door open from the outside corridor.

"Stop it, Tom." I give him a hard push. "It's the maid."

Footfalls across the carpeted floor come closer, then the door I'm leaning against pushes me tighter against Tom. Oh, brother.

A woman's face appears from around the doorjamb. "Am I interrupting a romantic interlude?" Drop-Dead-Gorgeous inquires.

As Tom's towel slips to the floor, I dash across the room.

"Well, I never expected this." The woman laughs.

By that time, I have grabbed my purse from the bed and scooted out the door. I race for the elevator with the speed of a fifty-year old—forget twenty, I left that behind eons ago.

I'm leaving. I cannot do this with Tom anymore.

But where will I go?

If I return to the states, the Russians will find me. If I stay here, I'll err for certain. Stay or go? What a dilemma!

* * *

Tom slips on his pants as Kelly Knotts unabashedly glares at his nudity. "Why did your girlfriend run? Is she a virgin?"

Tom frowns. "Dorothy's not used to all of this."

"Heavens, I hope she never is," Kelly pipes as she backs out of the way so Tom can pass through the open bathroom door.

"Twice in one day; why the sudden visit?" He'd told her he would not return to America yet or stray from his original goal.

"Does this mean you're on my side?" He asks.

Kelly plops down on the bed. "The jury is still out," she says. "Sit, Tom. There are some things you need to know."

Kelly's face is angelic. Her actions in real life—not so much. But God will judge greater sinners than Kelly as time unwinds.

He slips on a Polo pullover and sits in a chair to tie his tennis shoes. "Okay, I'm listening. Make it quick. I need to find Dorothy before she does something stupid like calling a cab for the airport."

Kelly pulls a thread on the bedcover. "Clyde Willems."

"Old news," Tom quips. "Dead and buried. Period."

"He wasn't stupid, you know . . ."

"The children's book." Tom nods.

"Yeah. That. Charlie phoned to see if I'd found you."

"And what did you say?"

"I'm still looking," Kelly replies.

"Good girl."

Kelly snickers. "You really like her."

Tom only glares.

"None of my business. I get that." She smacks her plumb lips.

"Say what you've come to tell me."

"Clyde was a redneck, serial gambler, but not stupid. He had friends in low places that fed him information about what Charlie was up to." Kelly rolls her neck and it snaps. "It was Charlie who sent Mark Hagen to Columbia to do his wet work."

"I figured," Tom says. "He took out Powell, Perkins, and Willems first. Hit the sister, Lorita. Killed Zoey Jackson's grandfather and later arranged for her to die—a suicide look-alike."

"But failed to eliminate Dorothy," Kelly notes, massaging the tight muscles in her neck while profusely yawning from jetlag.

"Not enough rest?" Tom walks over to the coffeemaker. "I'll fix us some strong brew. We both could use a jolt of caffeine."

"Why Dorothy?" She walks over and massages Tom's shoulders. "You're tight, G-man. I've taken a shine to you."

He shrugs off Kelly's hands and turns around. Her expression is priceless. She's not used to rejection. "Really, Kelly?"

"What's the matter? I'm not appealing enough?"

"No, but you're young enough to be my granddaughter. I would feel guilty if I ruined your reputation." Tom huffs.

"And *she* could be your mother!" Kelly scoffs, wounded to the core. "You know I'm not a virgin. Never been married. And won't."

"I'm not you, Kelly. I faithfully loved my wife."

"That's why you replaced her with Dorothy."

Tom sets the coffeemaker to doing its thing.

"Tell me what you really want; I need to move on."

"Did you know Clyde tried to blackmail Charlie?"

This is news. His thoughts circled around her statement.

"So, Clyde realized his days were numbered. He didn't want to go straight to the feds," Tom concludes. "That's why he coded the children's book. He wanted Arthur Powell to contact the feds."

"Exactly! Charlie plans on disappearing after he's collected enough money to live on for the rest of his life. But shit happens."

"Tell me about it."

Kelly fixes her coffee with cream and sugar. "Thanks." A toast to Tom and she takes several sips. "I needed this."

"Most of the scenario I've already figured out, Kelly.

"Jack wants you to come in and testify against Charlie." Kelly refers to their boss, U.S. CIA Director Jackson Carlton.

"I will, but not yet." Tom glares at Kelly. "I still need to move all of the drug funds out of Charlie's reach."

"What about Dorothy?"

"I'll see that she gets home safely."

Kelly laughs.

"What?"

"She'll never be safe. The Russians have long memories. Besides, she's old. Can't have too many natural years left."

Tom frowns. He doesn't like to think about that. His proposal of marriage was genuine, though Dorothy shot it down.

"Call Jack. Tell him I'll be in touch." He takes the mug from Kelly and shoves her out the door. "Goodbye."

* * *

I am sitting in the public park a few blocks from the Parisian Hotel contemplating my next move. Should I use Daphanie Daniel's creds and fly home? Or sit here and wait for Tom to find me?

He will eventually call. I am key to his nefarious plans.

A homeless man sits down on the park bench with me—at the other end, of course. He's a downer and I'm a what—an upper?

He opens a newspaper and scribbles something. I try not to look. But when he passes the paper over to me, I become suspicious.

He's not here by accident.

Who is he?

My phone dings and I dig it out of my expensive purse.

"Don't answer that," the homeless guy says as he inches closer to me on the bench. "I'm not who you think."

"Why not? I don't know you." I prepare to run.

"Read my note."

He's CIA.

"Really?"

"This is your chance to go home, Dorothy. We'll forget about your criminal activities with our CIA rogue. Cooperate and testify against Thomas Kessler and your troubles will all end. *Comprehende?*"

I know what that means in Spanish.

"I'll think about it." My phone continues to ding.

"Don't miss your chance, Ms. Powell."

I turn away from the stranger. "Tom? What a surprise!"

"Where are you?"

"At the park."

"Stay put, I'll come and pick you up. We're leaving."

"I'll meet you at the west corner." I end the call and look at the agent. "Give me your card, I'll think about your offer."

The homeless CIA agent walks in the opposite direction from me. I wonder if I should tell Tom about the offer. He's certainly keeping secrets from me. I'll ask him what Drop-Dead-Gorgeous had to say. If he levels with me, maybe I'll tell him about Jim Grossman.

11

Back in Tennessee

"CLAIRE, THIS IS LORENE." She waits for a response.

"Good morning," Claire says. "What's up?"

"I called to tell you that Dorothy phoned me a little while ago."

"Is she okay?"

"She sounded okay," Lorene replies.

"She was kidnapped, may I remind you."

"Dorothy didn't sound under duress," Lorene recalls. "I think your mother enjoys all of this clandestine stuff, and she loves Tom."

"Thomas Kessler." Claire sighs. "What exactly did Mama say?"

"She has a boatload of drug money and Tom wants to marry her," she reports. "She wears Prada shoes and carries a Gucci purse."

"Damn!" Claire curses. "My mother is nuts."

Lorene could not disagree.

* * *

Captain Marilyn Colbert needed a break from the office, so she is seated with Detective Galena Chico at Coffee Call, the location where Gloria Bolton received her "latte to die for," as the editor of the Columbia Gazette had so aptly put it for their readers.

The story had gone international. Reports were still coming in from all over the world, sightings of the mysterious server who delivered the dose of death. The CIA reward is most generous.

"Venezuela?" Galena jerks. "Someone found Danny Mason?"

"Yes. For the reward money, of course."

"Here all the time we thought he was dead."

Marilyn leans forward. "The body found in Mason's apartment in Crossville was a look-alike, so we searched no further."

"What about DNA evidence?"

"The hair on his comb matched Mason's."

"So, maybe the dead man is a relative?"

"Or the DNA was planted," Marilyn replies.

Galena nods. "The Russians got Mason out of Dodge."

"Exactly!" the captain replies, sipping on her vanilla latte. "As the nephew of the former drug lord of Kentucky, Mason has clout."

"So, Zoey Jackson's murder case?"

"Unsolved. The boyfriend has a concrete alibi. Two friends vouch they were with him the night Zoey took her life," Marilyn reports. "Dorothy Powell never bought the college girl's suicide."

"Any idea where our Nancy Drew is hiding out?"

"Not at this time."

"I don't like loose ends," Galena admits. "What about Mason? Maybe he came to Columbia to get paid twice."

"You think he murdered Zoey?"

This is a new wrinkle in Marilyn's brain.

"I don't rule any possibilities out," says Galena.

Marilyn nods. "We know Dom had her taken her out of the states when she betrayed him. If Detective Peters and Ellie Simpson had not rescued her, no telling where she'd be today."

"I think when Mason's extradited to the U.S., we need to look at him for both murders," Galena says. "I want to close both cases."

"Who doesn't?" Marilyn fingers the server to bring their check.

They part ways outdoors. As Galena gets in her truck, she sees a message blinking on her cell phone. She takes a look. Claire Burkes has called. Galena returns the call. "Did you call, Ms. Burkes?"

"Claire, please."

"Okay, Claire. How may I assist you?" Galena starts the engine.

"My mother phoned Lorene Perkins earlier today."

With scattered thoughts, Galena spins the truck around in the middle of the highway and heads north on Highway 7.

"Are you still there?" Claire inquires.

"I'm on my way to talk to Ms. Perkins. I need her phone."

"You think you can trace the call?" Claire does not doubt technology has exponentially leaped in the past twenty years.

"Did Ms. Perkins report anything interesting?"

"Mama said she was safe, that Thomas Kessler asked for her hand in marriage," Claire says. "Do you think he forced her to call?"

"You believe Dorothy was under duress when they spoke?" Dorothy's marrying a man young enough to be her son seems preposterous to Galena. "Let's see where the call leads us."

"Thank you. All I want is for Mama to safely come home."

"We all want that, Ms. Burkes."

"What if she called on a prepaid phone?"

"My friend at TBI will assist in the process," Galena says. "The feds have more sophisticated programs than our local police force."

"I certainly hope so," Claire spouts.

"Anything else you want to tell me?"

"No, just that my mother is eighty-three-year-old, and I worry about her mental stability to continue coping with the situation."

Galena chuckles. "Are you sure she's not up to it?"

Claire nervously laughs. "You're right. Mama's having a ball."

* * *

Lorene bawls while sitting on her front porch steps as Galena pulls her truck in the circle driveway and gets out. She waves the detective over, sniffling while drying her tears with the hem of her blouse. "Claire phoned you," Lorene concludes. "How can I help?"

Galena sits beside Dorothy's best friend on the step.

"What time did Dorothy call?"

"My time or her time?" Lorene looks at the detective.

"Any background noises indicating the time of day?"

"Morning, I think. She mentioned just having breakfast. She wears Prada shoes and carries a Gucci purse. Is that important?"

Galena thinks about Dorothy's situation. "You think she really loves her abductor and is seriously considering marrying him?"

"Clint Howard—I mean Tom—always had her attention. She pined over him even when she believed he might be dead," Lorene babbles on. "He took a bullet for Dorothy, you know."

"May I borrow your phone for the afternoon?" Galena inquires.

"Sure. But if either of my sons call, answer it. Okay?"

"How about I give you a burner and you call them—tell them why you don't have your cell phone." Galena gives her a prepaid phone. "I'd better take your cell to my tech guy and call my TBI friend for his assistance." That done, she drives away in her truck.

12

IT IS LATE AFTERNOON in France when the private jet lifts off the tarmac carrying Tom, me, and our newest bestest friend, Keleana.

The beautiful CIA agent is sleeping at the back of the plane.

"I don't know why we had to bring her along," I complain.

He winks a smile. "We need a witness when we get married."

I roll my shoulders, dip my head, and glare at my companion.

"I never agreed to marry you," I remind him.

"I don't need a verbal. I see how you look at me."

I fist him in the shoulder hard.

"Ouch! What was that for?"

"Playing with my emotions. Sure, I love you. But I love a lot of things. I love playing Canasta. I love my daughter. I love my—"

Tom is kissing me before I know it. His lips linger far too long for me to protest my devotion for him. I am such an old fool.

"How was that, honey?" He hands me a plastic ring from a package of Cracker Jacks. "You know what this means."

I laugh. "You have persuasive ways, I must admit."

He pops the lid to a Coke and hands it to me. "I'm serious about marrying you, Daphanie. We are quite a team together."

"A wife cannot testify against her husband."

"My feelings are hurt." He mimics a sad face.

"I don't know about a team, but we're also dead criminals if the Russian mob finds us. They must know we're stealing their funds." A sip of Coke explodes in my mouth with pleasure. "Thanks."

"For the kiss or the Coke?"

"Both." I smile. "About Kelly—what's her beef with you?"

"Director Carlton sent her to find me and bring me in," Tom replies as he yanks his neck to one side and it cracks.

Arthur used to do that.

"You said no to her and she agreed?"

"No, I offered her a piece of our pie."

"The money." I nod. Is life always about love or the love of money? I think both are driving forces in people's lives.

He nods, no comment.

"You never said where this plane is taking us."

"Someplace interesting," he replied. "We need to withdraw funds from a bank located in the Cayman Islands."

"We? You mean me."

"You are Daphanie."

"Stupid Daphanie," I qualify.

It seems we're in a big hurry to abscond all the money as fast as we can. Tom must believe that Charlie Darby is onto his game. He was a clever double-agent and didn't get this far, otherwise.

"You said *need,* Tom. Is this our last withdrawal?"

"Depends . . ." Tom grins.

"You always double-speak. I'm not your patsy."

He laughs. "I love how you've caught onto the lingo of a criminal," he says and I want to slap him. I'm a good Methodist.

He can tell I'm peeved at his assessment of me.

"Look. If we are successful with this one last gig, you can go home. Promise." Then he whispers in a sexy voice, "Unless you really want to spend the rest of your life with me—probably on a large yacht sailing the distant seas. We can make love twice a day."

I drool over that kind of life. Rich. Every convenience at my fingertips. The man I love, all to myself. Heaven on earth.

Wake up, Dorothy! I slap my face to reality.

And for a moment I look around a room and do not know where I am. Confusion sets in. I want to go back to my Tom.

"Dorothy?" he calls my name.

And the room dissolves.

"What? Sorry, a senior moment." I am so close to saying yes to Tom's proposal I am shaking in my skin. But luckily Drop-Dead-Gorgeous plops down in a seat behind me and Tom.

"What's going on? Where are we headed?"

"It's a need-to-know thing, Kelly," I quip. "If we tell you, we'll have to kill you. I don't think that will bring happiness to your young life with so many possibilities in front of you." I shrug.

Tom laughs. "You're too much, baby."

"I'm not your baby, Tom. Don't call me that."

Kelly snickers. "He really likes you. That's a huge surprise."

I look at the young CIA agent and want to choke her. She's got her whole life ahead of her, and what? I don't. We'll see about that.

"I need to use the little girl's room," I tell Tom.

He jacks a thumb, pointing to the back of the jet.

The wind is whipping the plane as I make my way down the aisle toward the back. Then a big jolt. Before I know it, Kelly has opened the back door to the plane and has me by the arm.

"Goodbye, trouble-maker!" She shoves me out of the plane.

I do not even have time to call out for help. I am falling through the air at an exponentially fast speed. I can't get my breath.

Is this it, Jesus? I just die?

≈

The next thing I know I am seated in a room that smells like death. A casket sets at the front. I wonder who is inside? I glance around and notice that I'm alone in the room. *Or am I?*

A presence sits down in the chair next to me.

I glance over. The guy is young, but he wears a white toga.

"Are you an angel?" I whisper to him.

"No. I AM."

That is an ambiguous answer, I think to myself.

"Oh . . . YOU are?"

"I AM." He smiles.

I meditate on that answer. If this is truly Jesus, God Incarnate, what is He doing here with me? I get up and walk over to the coffin.

The face staring back at me is familiar. It's my face.

The Presence stands quietly beside me.

"Is this a dream?" I wonder which direction I'm about to go— up or down? I haven't been the most devoted Methodist in the world. I wait patiently for His answer. He looks serious.

"We're all in God's dream, Dorothy."

≈

"Ouch!" I open my eyes and look around. The room with the coffin and Jesus is no longer here. I am lying on the floor.

"Get up, Dorothy, and make me breakfast."

I peek over the end of my bed.

Is this my house?

If it is, Ellie Simpson no longer owns it—which means time has backtracked. That doesn't make a shred of sense to me.

Wait! I am dead. I saw the coffin with me in it.

But Arthur only stands over me, laughing.

"You fell out of bed, honey." He grabs my hand and pulls me to my feet. "Did you hurt yourself bad?"

I shake my head, totally confused.

"What day is it?"

"Monday," he replies.

"What month?"

"October."

His answer starts to worry me.

"What's the exact date, Arthur?"

"It's Monday, October 24th. Sure you're okay?"

I dig a finger in one ear as I try to make sense of what is happening—why I am here. Is this the flashback everybody gets when they die? Am I still in God's dream, or is this really happening?

"Get up, Dorothy, and make me breakfast," Arthur tells me. "I have to gather the eggs from the barn and feed the cows."

"Wait!" I have a ton of questions.

But he's already left our bedroom.

I sit down on the edge of the bed to think about what to do next. I can make breakfast . . . or I can go over and talk to Lorene about my dilemma. If everything I did with Clint Howard/Thomas Kessler was only a dream, should I worry that Arthur will die today?

Or is Jesus punishing me for not being a good Methodist? And this is my version of Hell. If not, I have to prevent everything I dreamed about from really happening. I have to save Arthur, and ultimately Lorene's husband Crawford from that awful Mark Hagen.

If everything I've experienced with Tom is only a dream, our husbands did not lend Clyde Willems money to pay off his gambling debts to the Russian drug lords. And Clyde's sister, Lorita Willems, is alive. Zoey Jackson is still breathing since she didn't double cross a hitman named Mark Hagen. Dom is not trying to kill me every day.

And Gloria Bolton did not die from a poison latte.

"Wow!" I enthusiastically say. "Thank you, Jesus! It's a relief to know everything that happened to me was a dream."

I feel a pump of renewed energy.

"Now, maybe I can relax and enjoy being an elderly person that likes playing cards with her friends and enjoys having my family around me. I will phone Claire to tell her how much I love her.

I wonder if I actually had a facelift.

A mirror will speak the truth.

But do I really want to know? Maybe I still look old. At that dismal thought, I prefer to believe that my dreams are actually true.

13

I KNOCK ON LORENE'S front door. I didn't call first before driving my old Cadillac over to her house. Forget about the expensive BMW I purchased when I dumped this one. She opens the door.

"Dorothy? What are you doing here?"

I push past her. "Is Crawford here?"

"Of course, he's here. It's barely 6:30. AM," she reminds me.

"I know, I know . . ." I throw a hand and head through the house toward the kitchen. "Do you have coffee made?"

I am suddenly needing a jolt of caffeine. I am so pleased that all that CIA clandestine stuff was only a nightmare. Now, I can relax and just enjoy my old age. I won't need a facelift because Arthur is two years older than me, and he thinks I'm still beautiful.

Lorene grabs a mug from the cabinet and fixes my coffee just like I enjoy it. "Thank you." I take a big swig. "I love you, Lorene."

"Are you feeling okay, Dorothy? You're acting strange."

"I'm fine, honestly." I take a seat at the breakfast bar.

Crawford limps into the kitchen and glares a me. I don't care, I am so happy to see him. I hug him like he's my long-lost best friend.

"Oh, Crawford, I'm so glad to see you this morning."

Embarrassed, he shoves be off and locks eye with Lorene.

I throw a hand. "I know, but I have an explanation."

"I gotta hear this," Crawford tells me.

Lorene makes breakfast for us while I tell them about my nightmare. "You see, it was only a dream. I have a second-chance at life to make it better. I can pray more. I can go every Wednesday to the united prayer meetings held at lunchtime. I promise never to miss Sunday School or a church service. I will be a model Christian."

"Goodness, Dorothy! You need a shrink!" Lorene exclaims. "Crawford? Call Arthur and tell him to come over right now."

"Is there enough breakfast for four?"

"Don't be silly, Crawford. Call your friend."

The four of us sit down at the dining table and enjoy country ham, scrambled eggs, and store-bought biscuits—but they're good.

Lorene opens a jar of blackberry jam and I smear real butter on my biscuit before adding an ample serving of jam. God is so good.

We finish breakfast and cozily sit together in the den.

Crawford asks Arthur, "Did Dorothy tell you about her dream?"

"No. But she fell out of bed this morning and hit her head on the floor," he replies. "I told her to make me breakfast while I checked the hens for fresh eggs. When I got back to the house, the Cadillac was missing. I presumed Dorothy had an errand to run."

"She did," Lorene says. "She came here. She told us about her awful nightmare. She believes you will be murdered by an assassin later today if she cannot stop Fate." Lorene shakes her head.

"What?" Arthur's gaze drifts on his wife.

"It gets worse," Lorene is on a roll, "Crawford will also be dead before a week is out." She grasps my hand. "Oh, sweetie . . ."

"You don't believe me, but what if my dream is prophetic?"

"Like a prophet in the Old Testament?" Crawford clarifies.

"Maybe my dream is a warning. God cares about us."

"Maybe it was only a nightmare," Arthur pipes.

"It could be prophetic," Lorene says, clearly on my side. That's what friends are for. I am not crazy. I only speak the truth.

"Okay, Dorothy, why don't you tell me how I die later today?"

I lock eyes on Arthur and take him through the whole scenario while Lorene and Crawford listen. They are frowning. And I do not like the way Arthur glares at me. He's worried I've lost my mind.

"Okay, guys, answer one question for me."

They nod their consent. Lorene just sits there.

"Have you loaned Clyde Willems money to pay off his gambling debts to Russian drug lords?" There, I've laid out the premise of my story. If they have, then everything I don't like is coming true.

"Yes or no!" I quickly quip, wanting reassurance.

The guys have locked eyes and look concerned.

"Tell her you didn't lend money to Clyde!" Lorene demands.

We are all silent as the Grim Reaper waltzes through the room.

"They can't, because it is true," I conclude. "I need to speak to Detective Galena Chico as soon as possible."

"Who is that?" Arthur inquires.

"Oh, I forgot. Butch is still breathing, so she has not taken his place yet." I get up and grab my purse from the bar. "I have to go."

"Wait, Dorothy! Where?" Lorene calls after me.

Two minutes later I am belted in my car and driving away before the cock crows three times. Before the Lord catches me in a lie, I will go over to Clyde's junky cabin and ask him directly if he gave a children's book to Arthur in August for his 82nd birthday.

And, Jesus, I will obey the speed limit.

I drive past my house and down the gravel road with a few potholes for three more miles. I recall the wonderful elderly woman who used to live here—well, in my dream, of course. I'll miss knowing Alicia Anderson Colby from Manchester, England.

If Clyde doesn't die, and Lorita doesn't contact Alicia and invite her to America, we will never meet. Why am I thinking about this?

It doesn't matter.

Or does it?

What if my dream is destined to come true? But, if God revealed the facts first, shouldn't I do everything possible to stop the flow of events that will bring death to so many people I know and love?

I never liked Clyde Willems. Actually, I thought he was a bad influence on Arthur and Crawford. So why am I going to see him? I stop in the middle of the road and think about my decision.

No, I tell myself, *I will see Clyde and ask him about the book.*

Clyde's old Ford truck is parked at his front door. I kill my motor—bad choice of words, Jesus. Then apologize. I waltz up to the front door, knock, and politely wait. He doesn't come.

As I turn around to leave, I hear my name called.

"Mrs. Powell? What are you doing here?"

I turn around to face Clyde. My heart goes out to him. Tears drip from my eyes. "Did something bad happen?" he inquires.

"No, Clyde. Not yet. But I need to talk to you."

"Sure. Come inside and I'll put on a pot of coffee."

I suddenly realize I am cold. It's a chilly October morning and the temperature has dipped into the fifties. I am not even wearing a jacket. Am I dead? Is this Hell? Is any of this real?

Now I am worried about my sanity. And for a nanosecond I am back in that small room with white walls. Alone and frightened.

But that vision doesn't last long.

Clyde has a fire built and it feels like Heaven. I sit in his old dusty recliner and think of all the beautiful furniture Alicia brought with her from England. I know Clyde could do better if he had more money. I'm an old fool. Why bother Clyde with a silly dream?

But it seems in my nature to search for a mystery and solve it.

Clyde returns to the living room, stokes the flaming wood, then hands me my mug of coffee. Dressed in jean overalls, he sits in a rocker across the room from me. He takes a sip of his Joe.

"Now, what can I do for you, Ms. Powell?"

"Dorothy, please. We are neighbors, after all."

"If you say so . . ."

"Clyde," I seriously ask, "do you have a gambling problem?"

"Did my sister Lorita send you here to interrogate me?"

"No, I've never met your sister. Does she live nearby?"

"Yes, in Dickson," he replies then takes a few more sips of his black brew. "To answer your question, I like to gamble."

I know he plays cards with Arthur and Crawford every Friday night like clockwork. "Do you owe bad people money?"

"What do you mean?" He sits forward, alert to my question.

I lean forward to probe his facial expressions and evaluate his sincerity. "Did you borrow money from my husband?"

I'll save the subject of Crawford for later.

"Why would you think that?" He glares at me.

Should I tell him about my dream?

"Let's just say, a little bird is spreading rumors," I respond.

"I don't recall borrowing any money," he spurts.

"So, you do not recall having a gambling problem, or borrowing money from my Arthur?" I want clarification.

"No."

"No, to which question?"

His mouth is clamped.

"I'm not your enemy."

"So, you say." I don't believe him. "I should go now."

I still don't know if Clyde gave a book to Arthur for his birthday shortly before a Russian assassin murdered him. But I've pushed this man about as far as I can without additional information.

I'm almost at the door when Clyde snags me by the elbow.

"Who sent you to interrogate me?"

I turn around, my tongue wagging for an answer. I'm surely not going to tell him the Russian drug lords. Or that I'm having memory problems. "Let go of me, Clyde!" I nearly shout at him.

He drops his hand. "Be careful asking questions like that, Ms. Powell. You can get into a whole lot of trouble that way."

Did he just threaten me?

14

AFTER LEAVING CLYDE'S cabin, I drove into town to see Detective Lloyd Peters. I pray he is still breathing, because if he isn't I am in a world of trouble. How will I know reality from a dream?

Ellie is seated at her desk typing a letter. She glances up.

"Ms. Powell! Did you have an appointment?"

"No, I need to see Butch."

Ellie frowns. She never liked me because I always put Lloyd down for his past behavior. I am ashamed of myself. *Jesus, forgive me!*

"I won't be long, Ellie. See if he'll give me a few minutes."

She walks over to the door to his private office and opens it.

"Lloyd, you have an unscheduled visitor."

Unscheduled, my eye! I laugh to myself.

Butch peeks around the doorjamb and motions for me to come inside his office. As usual, his desk is messy with open folders.

"What is it, Dorothy?"

No respect. He is curt with me. I understand. We have a jaded history. Before my prophetic dream, I despised him for feeling up my young Claire. I state my reason for interrupting his busy life.

"I'm here to apologize."

He snickers. "For what? Being you?"

"I wanted you to know that I'm truly sorry for the way I've treated you all these years. You had an awful childhood. Your father beat you—although you probably deserved it," I add, earning myself no points. "I also forgive you for nearly raping Claire while you were both in high school." I pause because he is laughing hard at me.

"Is something funny, Detective?"

"Is this a joke?" he asks. "Did Ellie pay you?"

"No, I'm being one-hundred percent sincere, Butch—I mean Lloyd. You don't like me calling you Butch. But I just want you to know I do not wish you any ill will. I pray you will have a long life."

"Ellie!" he calls out to his secretary.

"Yes?"

"Escort Ms. Powell to her car and sit with her. I will phone Arthur and ask him to come and get his insane wife."

"Wait, Lloyd! I'm not nuts. There's much you do not know."

He waves me off and closes the door to his office. I look at Ellie and can't help from frowning. "Never mind, I know my way out."

I take the elevator down to the first floor and exit the building. So much for honesty! Nobody wants to hear the truth from me.

I am weary by now and drive home. Arthur is there, waiting for me, just sitting calmly on the sofa with the TV turned down low.

I toss my purse on the kitchen table.

"Did you tend to the cattle?" I ask, desiring normal.

"I can do that later," he tells me. "What's wrong with you?"

I sit down, weary to the bone.

"The dream I had last night bothers me, Arthur. It was so real I fear the awful stuff in it will come true. Is that insanity?"

"I don't know, Dorothy. I'm not a psychiatrist."

"You think I should talk to somebody about my dream?"

"Do you want to? Is this a late, mid-life crisis?"

"Lord, no! I'm way past menopause."

Arthur chuckles. I will miss him if he dies.

"Sit down beside me, Dorothy. Let's try to sort out what's bothering you. Sometimes dreams have deeper meanings."

"Like, uh, it symbolizes something?"

"Yes, but what do I know about dream therapy?"

"Will you answer one question for me?"

"What?" Arthur grasps my hand. "Sure, honey."

"Did you lend Clyde Willems money because he has a gambling problem?" I study him for an honest answer.

"Why would you think such a thing?"

"In my dream, you did. And he gave you a children's book for your last birthday," I tell him. "It contained coded words."

He chuckles. "Sounds pretty clandestine to me, Dorothy. Maybe you've been reading too many spy novels, or watching too many crime movies. You have a big imagination. Maybe you should write a novel." He looks at me. "I mean it. You're just bored."

I'm glad he didn't say old and bored. But what he said made sense. People fantasize in dreams. Maybe I'm only normal.

"So, it's settled. We put the dream to bed?"

"But . . ." I hold up my right forefinger and shake it at Arthur, "what if my dream starts coming true? Maybe it's God's way of warning us what is about to happen. Can people change their fates?"

He shakes his head. "Answering that is above my paygrade."

"All I want to do is keep people alive, Arthur. A lot of good people got murdered in my dream," I reveal. "I'm worried."

He lets go of my hand. "So . . . I die in your dream?"

I nod, tears clouding my vision.

"Are you that bored with me, Dorothy?"

"No, of course not, Arthur."

He places his hands on his knees and gets up.

"Where are you going?" I ask.

"I need to cut the hay on the field down by Crystal Creek so it can get bailed tomorrow," he tells me. "I had a big breakfast so I'm skipping lunch." He picks up his jean jacket and old straw hat.

"I wish you wouldn't do that today, Arthur."

"Why is today so important? It's just another Monday."

"No, it isn't just another day. It's October 24th."

But he leaves the house anyhow.

I sit another few minutes thinking. Then realize I've not talked to my daughter about my premonition. I use the landline to call her.

"Claire? This is your mother. Are you busy this afternoon?"

* * *

She is at my house by one o'clock. The minutes are ticking by far too fast. I want to scream at the sun to slow down. If Arthur dies late this afternoon—no, is murdered by the Russian assassin, Mark Hagen—that means Crawford Perkins will be dead within a week. I don't have much time to alter Fate—if that is even possible.

"What troubles you, Mama?"

"Claire, I know this sounds crazy. But today is the beginning of a chain of events that will change all of our lives."

15

CLAIRE DROVE ME TO the clinic to see Dr. Robert Hammons, my primary physician. After hearing most all of my bizarre story she is convinced that I am having a nervous breakdown.

"No, I will talk to him alone," I insist.

"Mama, I want to hear everything that is said."

"You don't trust me. You think I am paranoid."

"No, I think you are confused and need special medication," Claire counters. "Be careful not to say too much."

"You think he'll call the little white men to take me to the Looney Zoo and lock me up, like forever?" My feelings are hurt.

"You have a tendency to overly emphasize the truth."

"I lie." The thought makes me laugh.

"But, if there is truly something wrong with you, it cannot be ignored," Claire continues. "I just hope that—"

"What? I don't have Alzheimer's or dementia?"

"Well, you are getting up in age."

"That's not it, Claire. If I've had a prophetic dream, I should not ignore it. God could be telling me something. A gift, I think."

"Mama, I just want to do right by you."

"Okay, I'll talk to Dr. Hammons, if only to please you," I say. "But I don't expect him to understand how my mind works."

Claire doesn't respond and that hurts my feelings.

I check in at the front desk and we sit down to wait for my name to be called. "Mama, are you happy living with Daddy?"

I look at my daughter. "That's a silly question, Claire. We've been married forever. Have I ever said I was unhappy?"

"No, but all this romance stuff in your dream—is it possible you don't feel loved enough?" Claire studies me for a response.

"I feel loved, Claire. June questions my sanity sometimes, but what does a five-year-old know about real life?"

"Dorothy Powell," the receptionist calls out my name.

Claire clasps my arm like I'm going to run away from her. I gently nudge myself free and walk through the open door and down the long hallway to Dr. Hammons' private office. He stands to greet us, a huge smile cracking his tired face. Claire is next to me.

"Come in, ladies. Fine morning. Great to see both of you."

I won't wait for Claire to speak for me. "Dr. Hammons. Thank you for seeing me on such short notice. I've had a strange dream and my family believes there are subconscious underlying circumstances I need to consider." I hope he understood what I just said, I don't.

"What I mean is, I need for you to tell me if I'm going insane."

"Mama!" Claire is horrified.

Dr. Hammons looks between me and Claire. Then back at me.

"Do you think you're losing a sense of reality, Dorothy?"

I smile at him. I like knowing my doctor sees me as a real person, not as an old lady with half her marbles gone—so to speak.

"Can you do a brain scan on Mama to see if anything's amiss?"

"We can, if I believe her condition warrants it," he replies.

"Don't you want to hear my dream?" I inquire.

"I study the physical body, Dorothy, not the mental or spiritual ones. I can recommend a good psychiatrist you can speak with."

"Maybe, but first will you examine my brain?"

"What if your insurance doesn't cover a scan?"

"She can pay," Claire answers for me.

"Okay. I'll send you over to the hospital for an MRI."

"Thank you, Dr. Hammons," Claire tells him.

He stands and pats me on the shoulder. "But if nothing shows up, and you still are bothered by your dream, call this number."

He hands me the name of a shrink: Dr. Emad Molieski.

A foreign doctor, I think. He will never understand the mind of an American woman—not one that is as elderly as I am.

Claire and I exit the clinic. "Want to get some lunch while we are in town?" she asks as we get into her Buick. "I'm hungry."

"Can we stop by the new facility and pick up Alicia Colby?"

"What new facility?" Claire starts the motor.

"Oh, yeah, I forgot. That was in my dream—there was the nicest lady that crossed the Atlantic and moved into Clyde Willems' cabin after he was murdered," I recall. "She fixed up the place. After Clyde's sister was murdered, she was targeted by the Russian Mafia."

"Mama, stop this!" Claire hits the brakes and I nearly bump my head against the dashboard. "None of that is true."

"How can you say that, she was in my dream?"

"Not one more word about a dream until we get your MRI report!" she counters with anger. "Are we perfectly clear?"

I burst out in tears. Nobody understands me. Or believes me. I am in big trouble. But, they will all be sorry when my dream comes true. We drive the rest of the way to the hospital in frantic silence.

* * *

We are back at my house by 4:13 p.m. Claire needs to go home, but she is coming inside the house first to make sure Arthur is there.

I snag my key from under the flower pot beside the backsteps to my porch, vowing never to sell my house under any circumstances.

Arthur's work shoes are parked at the back door. I use my key to let Claire in first and follow her like an obedient child. My husband is seated on the sofa, wearing his work overalls, snoring gourds.

"Wake up, Arthur!" I nudge him.

"Huh? Uh, Dorothy." He looks at Claire. "Everything okay?"

"We don't know," I answer for her. "I had an MRI scan of my brain—Dr. Hammons will call me tomorrow with a report," I tell him. "We had a nice lunch at Bart's BBQ. Food was super."

He rolls his shoulders and stands up. "Now that you are home, I need to drive the cows over to the other pasture," he says.

"Not by Crystal Creek?" I nearly scream.

"Mama thinks someone will try to kill you tonight," Claire says.

"It was in my dream, Arthur. Forget about the cows tonight." I think if we can change just one thing, everything else will not happen.

That also means Clint Howard won't come to town to oversee the operation of the Senior Citizen Center. And I will never learn that he is actually an undercover CIA agent. Or fall head-over-heels in love with him—a man that is young enough to be my son.

Does that distress me?

"Mind staying with your mother while I tend to the cows?" Arthur queries Claire. "I should be back before suppertime."

"Don't go, Arthur. Please!" I beg him.

He gives me a hug. "I'll be fine, Dorothy."

"But what if you aren't?"

"I wish I could stay, Daddy, but Ted and I have made dinner plans with the kids. It's Benjamin's birthday and Helen wants to surprise him." She looks at me. "Of course, you are invited, Mama."

I smirk. *No, I wasn't.* This is news to me.

He puts on his hat and follows her out the backdoor.

After both have left the house, I am alone and feeling despondent. I find my Bible in the bedroom and open it to Psalm.

"Lord," I lift up a prayer, "I am so sorry for being such a selfish Christian! If I could live my life all over again, I'd do it differently."

Then I sit in Arthur's chair and dread how I will feel if he never sits here again. Life seems so brief now that I'm looking back over the decades. I even feel more tender toward Detective Butch. And I will forgive Claire for not inviting me to Ben's birthday party.

After reading a passage of scripture penned by King David, I open the novel I checked out of the library. It's all about crime.

Time goes by. Ten minutes. Thirty. One hour.

I fix supper just like I've done every other Monday evening since Arthur and I have owned our 1934 two-story farmhouse on 200 acres of prime fertile land. When he is not home by six, I start to worry.

By 6:30 p.m. I am in a tizzy. Then there is a knock at my front door. It sends my blood pressure into the Twilight Zone. If I answer it, will Clyde Willems be standing there? Will he tell me that Arthur has had an accident? That he fell and hit his head on a rock?

The knock persists. I cannot ignore Fate any longer.

I traipse through the kitchen and down the hall toward the front of the house. My dining room furniture is on my left as always. I glance up the stairs from the foyer and know I have three bedrooms and a bath on the second level. I stand before the door, terrified.

The knock persists.

Bang! Bang! Bang!

The sound grows louder, more ominous.

BANG! BANG! BANG!

"No!" I scream. "I won't open it! Go away! NO, NO, NO!"

16

Sunday, July 16

I AM COLD AS MY eyes slowly open to a rude awakening.

"It's okay, honey, I'm right here."

The room around me is spinning. My throat feels parched. I know I am not lying on white desert sand because the soil beneath me feels like a soft cushion. The air blows cold across my face.

Deserts are hot. I try to focus my eyes but can't.

Where am I?

"It's okay, Dorothy, I'm right here. You've had an accident."

I try to sit up but fail. My muscles feel as weak as jelly.

"Where am—" I try to speak but my voice is raspy.

"You are in a hospital," the answer comes back.

I open one eye and squeak out one word. "Where?"

"Hell."

My eyes fly open and I force myself to sit up.

"Hell! I knew it. That explains everything!"

Then the room goes dark again.

* * *

Ellie Simpson's parents, Wes and Jasmine, are away on a cruise in Europe. She'd spoken with Lorene Perkins and learned that an agent with the Tennessee Bureau of Investigation has traced Dorothy's prepaid cell phone call to a cell tower in France. Dorothy always said she wanted to travel abroad, but this was not a scheduled trip. It is believed that CIA Thomas Kessler had kidnapped her.

Ellie dresses and leaves the house that once belonged to the Powell's. She has read the New Testament gifted her by Dorothy and has decided going to church to hear one Christian sermon will not damage her position with God—if there really is only one true deity.

Certainly, there is a Creator because nothing else makes sense. How can one flaming star be positioned so perfectly in the universe that it gives light and heat to the earth to nourish all kinds of life?

No, there is more to this life that flesh and blood.

Ellie chose to visit the First Methodist Church that morning, although Lorene had argued that First Baptist would be a better choice. You could get saved without worrying about doing a lot of works. She thought that was a silly difference, that maybe Lorene misunderstood what the Word of God actually meant: that when one is loyal to a cause, one will work their fanny off to please.

She is driving an old Chevrolet built back in the 60s that she recently purchased. Lloyd Peters had always wanted to collect old cars so she had begun the task to please him beyond the grave.

"Butch! I hope you're looking down from Heaven."

* * *

Lorene is also on her way to Columbia to attend Sunday School at Dorothy's church, hoping to learn more about her friend's disappearance. Graham and Cynthia are sleeping in this morning. New dads and moms need a day of rest—just like the Lord Jesus prescribed, but no family should live their lives without honoring God. Little Graham would need to hear the Ten Commandments taught in order to grow up to be a moral, God-fearing man.

Dorothy's ninety-year-old Sunday School teacher died last week so Elizabeth Hinson is teaching the Bible lesson this morning. There are only eight members left in their senior class. Four died during the Covid outbreak. Lorene uses the side entrance to the impressive 1965 brick church building funded by a millionaire who no longer lives in Columbia. Dorothy's classroom is located in the basement toward the front of the church where there is a window to let in natural light.

Old folks need lots of light to lift their moods. She takes a seat next to Charlie Bark, owner of Bark's BBQ in the heart of Columbia.

"How are you doing this morning, Charlie?"

"Little trouble with arthritis, but other than that . . ."

The way Charlie let the word 'that' linger makes Lorene wonder if something else ails him. He returns, "You?"

"Can't complain, but I'm awfully worried about Dorothy Powell. I suppose you've heard she's been missing since July the fourth."

"Yeah, gossip came my way the day after it happened. You two were mighty close," he says. "You think she's dead?"

"Who can say what Fate dishes out?" She'd promised not to talk about Dorothy's phone call. A tear slides down one cheek.

"Good morning, Class," Lizzy Hinson addresses the group. "I was asked to teach the lesson this morning." She stands bent at a lectern—a little shaky and somewhat nervous.

"Good morning, Lizzy," class members respond.

"Well, I'll get right to it—we are studying the Book of Jonah." She reads the Bible scripture and brings out the main points.

Thirty minutes goes by pretty quickly since Lorene has barely internalized one word. She keeps thinking about Charlie's question.

You think she's dead?

* * *

The sunlight shines brightly through the window as I open my eyes. I don't think Hell has any light, so I wonder where I really am.

No one is in the room with me. A cold substance drips through a clear tube into the vein of one arm. I recall someone telling me that I was in an accident. Is this a hospital room? It must be.

I feel around in the bedsheets and find the gizmo that allows me to call a nurse. I press a button and wait. Three people wearing white garb rush into the room. Tom Kessler is right behind them.

Double S-S! I hiss to myself. I am still in my nightmare.

"You're awake." Tom comes closer and grasps my hand. "We were so worried about you. Do you remember anything before you passed out?" He looks down at me. "You fell and hit your head."

My thoughts are still foggy but I recall I was on a plane headed for the Cayman Islands. "You said *we*; who is we?"

"Me." Drop-Dead-Gorgeous appears in the doorway.

By now, a nurse has disconnected my tubing and is insisting I drink some juice. I ignore her, sit up, and point my finger.

"She threw me out of the plane!" I refer to Kelly Knotts.

"No, Dorothy," Tom counters. "You're confused."

"I'm not confused about *her!*" I am ballistic.

"Listen to logic, please! We were flying in a plane when you removed your seatbelt and started moving down the aisle. When the plane hit an air pocket, you took a dive, fell, and hit your head."

"When?" I try to put together the pieces stirring in my brain.

"On Thursday, July 13," Tom replies.

"What day is it?" I push myself up, then fall back, very weak.

"Sunday, July 16th. You've suffered a concussion and been in a coma since Thursday. Another day here and they'll dismiss you."

"You said we were in Hell."

"We are!" Kelly snaps, glaring at me.

I don't like this CIA agent. Nor do I trust her as far as I can throw her. And that isn't far, since I'm weak as running water.

"Hell, Grand Cayman," Kelly clarifies our location.

"Then I must've been dreaming," I tell Tom. "It was so real. I saw Arthur and it was the day he was murdered. You never were in Columbia," I reveal. "Jesus told me we're all in God's dream."

Tom's lips curl into a smile.

"Well, I'm here now, Dorothy. And this is real."

Is it? I am not convinced. *A dream within a dream?*

"Are we still going to steal Charlie Darby's stash?"

"You bet we are," Kelly answers.

I glare at the dutiful CIA agent—too young to appreciate life, and I do not trust her meddling in *our* business. She's betraying us.

17

Monday, July 17

BANKS ARE OPEN IN the Grand Cayman Islands. I am fully awake and in charge of my mental faculties. For the past forty-five minutes, I've been reading about the three sister islands on the internet and understand why so many wealthy internationals desire to live here.

The main island encompasses 264 square kilometers. Its sister islands, Caman Brac and Little Cayman, are smaller. There are peaks of limestone mountains that reach 155 feet high, and 99 miles of pristine coastline on all three islands. Banking is private and rich people love that, so they flock here to open accounts and deposit their funds sometimes earned from illegal means—like Agent Charlie Darby's account. I am going to see that he does not keep his stash.

"Good morning!" I greet Keleana with a lilt in my voice.

She grunts, ignores me, and heads for the coffeemaker.

Not so friendly with me, I note her arrogance.

Tom is seated at the breakfast bar reading a local newspaper. He looks up and winks at me. "Give the girl a break."

I shrug. I'd like to give her a break. In the leg, so we can send her home to the CIA gurus and let them deal with her testiness.

Kelly eyes me then sits down next to Tom. Too close for my comfort. This girl has a crush on my man. Is that what he is to me?

Do I really know him?

He swept into Columbia more than two years ago and went after my heart like a scavenger devouring a cadaver. I thought he was Clint Howard, a man who had lost his wife and needed a friend. He seemed nice, employed by the city to run the Senior Citizen Center. I could not imagine he had a devious bone in him, so I was more than willing to bolster his confidence in older women. After all, not many handsome, intelligent men move into my hometown and pay attention to me. Then I learned he was far more than he seemed.

I was chosen since I resembled his deceased wife. Clint Howard, a.k.a. CIA Agent Thomas Kessler, seduced me for that very reason.

Angela was beautiful, he told me. But until recently, I had no idea she was a former Russian spy working with CIA Agent Charlie Darby to undermine the goals of our American government.

Tom also admitted that Angela turned on the Russians when they fell in love and she married him. It was Angela who had set up the foreign accounts where drug lords deposited their money.

Except her given name was Daphanie Daniels.

I fell in love with Tom almost immediately.

What lonely widow wouldn't?

He was debonaire, smart, sexy, and captured my heart like the pirate he is most of the time. Does he really want to marry me?

Am I free to leave at any time, or his permanent captive?

Those answers stump me since I want to believe in my lifelong dream of an exciting life while traveling around the world in style.

But now that I am aware of his agenda, is he trustworthy?

He tells me I am safe with him.

But am I really?

And who is Keleana really? Is she loyal to Charlie Darby and not Tom? Is she still on the Russian payroll? Maybe she's Charlie's young lover. Afterall, she found us and traces our every move.

I'm not happy with the situation.

"I see that mind working." Tom puts down the newspaper, gets up from the round table by the window and saunters over to the bar.

I'm on the other side of the counter sipping my Kona brew, rolling my tight shoulders because I am stressed.

Shall I answer him truthfully?

"Cat got your tongue this morning?" His strong hands grasp the edge of the bar, supported by forearms muscling up through his Island tan. I cannot help but smile at him. I am a pushover.

"Just thinking over the past few years—how I've come so far away from who I used to be." The truth stabs me in the heart.

He reaches across the bar and grasps my forearm.

I should pull away and tell him to take a hike, but I don't.

Aw, such is true love. It forgives and bears no ill will.

Kelly notices we're having a moment and abandons her seat.

"I'm getting packed," she issues with malice.

"I don't think that girl likes me."
He laughs. "She's just jealous. She knows we're together."
I don't feel very together so I do not comment.
He notices my reaction.
"Is something wrong, Dorothy? Have I offended you?"
"Kelly's packing, does that mean we're leaving the island today?"
He drops in a barstool at the counter, glaring at me.
"This was never meant to be a vacation."
"You break my heart." I feign hurt.
"All right. What is your good pleasure?"
That leaves me with a lot of options.
"I just woke up, Tom. As far as I am concerned, we just arrived. I want to do some sight-seeing before we depart Paradise."
"We have the morning," he says. "I'll show you around Hell."
"I've already been there and back." I recall my dream.
"Did something bad happen while you were in a coma?"
"No, something good happened. You are my Hell."
Hurt settles in his gaze. "I see you're not wearing my ring."
"Oh, that." I glare at the finger that once bore a plastic ring.
"Yes, *that*. Are we still engaged?"
"Arthur gave me a diamond and you give me a ring from a box of Cracker Jack's?" I make my point. "Someone else took it off."
He grins. "That's good to know. It means you still love me."
"That's debatable." I won't bolster his confidence today.
"We're visiting a branch of the Grand Island Bank today."
"When?" I replenish my coffee cup at the counter. Taking my time, I add cream and sugar before turning around to face Tom.
"Three o'clock this afternoon," he replies.
"You said *we*. You mean *me*. I am visiting a bank today."
"Yes, same routine as before except the account number is not recorded in the little black book you removed from the First Federal Bank in Knoxville," he informs me. "Come sit down with me at the table and I'll explain how important today is to all concerned."
I do not know *Who All* concerned is, but my butt is on the line.

* * *

Back in Columbia, Detective Chico receives a call from her contact at TBI and listens carefully to a report concerning Danny Mason, the young man who murdered Gloria Bolton by mistake.

Her widower Gerry has been leaving messages all morning after reading about Danny's arrest in Argentina last week. The Nashville paper can't keep the news quiet. Her desk phone rings.

"Yes, Blake?"

"Gerry Bolton is here to see you. He says he's not leaving until you talk to him. What do you want me to do, boss?"

"Don't call me boss, for starters. Send him in."

Galena opens her office door and locks eyes on the elderly man. He looks ragged and hasn't shaved for days. "I was going to call you." She motions for him to take a seat in the fold-out metal chair.

"When? Christmas?"

Galena smacks her lips. "Sooner than that."

"So, you say. . ." Gerry's in no mood to put up with incompetency. The police force needs to do its job and report to those concerned in a timely matter.

"What can I do for you today?"

"I read where they found Danny Mason. I thought he died."

"We all thought wrong," Galena says. "Mason will be in custody by tomorrow—here in the Columbia City Jail," she informs him.

"I hope the local police have not been careless."

Galena took in a quick breath. "Finding your wife's killer has been a long time in coming, Mr. Bolton. But not for lack of trying. Mason will pay for his crime." She sits at her desk. "Want a coffee?"

He nods. It's barely 8:30 a.m. and he skipped breakfast.

Galena buzzes Blake. "Go over to Coffee Call and pick up three lattes with an order of pastries." She looks at Gerry. "What kind?"

"Doesn't matter."

"Any coffee flavor preference?"

"Plain." Like his soul feels today.

"Have you located Dorothy Powell yet?" he inquires.

"I cannot comment on an ongoing investigation."

He nods. "Par for the course."

"How have you been, Mr. Bolton?"

"Take a look and me—that's all you need to know."

"Do you have any particular questions regarding Mason?"

"No, but I'd like an update on Dorothy's whereabouts."

"So would we," Galena shoots back. "Considering your past experience with Ms. Powell, I'm surprised you even speak of her."

"We're past Gloria's death. And have become friends. Loosely. She's lost a lot, too. And she did not kill Gloria. They were rivals in high school, but that was a long time ago," he reports.

"Very noble of you, Mr. Bolton."

"I'm not one to hold grudges. Call me Gerry, please." He relaxes a bit. "Can you tell me how Danny Mason was found in Argentina?"

"I'll tell you what's not classified."

"What was his beef with Dorothy?"

"What I have to say is not to be passed on. Are we clear?"

"Yeah, we're clear."

"I hope what I tell you will ease your mind." She began way back when Arthur Powell was first murdered near Crystal Creek.

18

WE LEFT OUR SUITE at the Kimton Seafire Resort and Spa and drove into Hell to visit the National Gallery. During our cab ride I spied street musicians playing the soul of jazz. Tom told me that islanders were joyful people, entrenched in a culture dating back too far to count. Hell held festivals throughout the year to celebrate various holidays and scheduled events. I felt happy, strangely.

I learned from a pamphlet that there were seven commercial galleries in the city. Artists' studios were in abundance. Islanders sold their paintings and crafts to the hundreds of yearly visitors.

After viewing multiple sights, we had a late lunch at one of the popular restaurants. The Tilapia, a fish served with a medley of homegrown vegetables I did not recognize, was delicious. Tom had the Lobster Thermador. We ate like there was no tomorrow.

Afterwards, we sat together on a park bench.

Tom prepped me for how to handle the bank manager when I closed Charlie Darby's account and transferred his funds. Now we were stealing the wolf's stash and somehow the idea thrills me. I'll never forgive Charlie for using his phone to copy the pages of the little black bank book when I wasn't looking. Hate runs deep.

Time has moved with warp speed. It's nearly 3:30 p.m.

"I know what to do, Tom," I tell him as the cab pulls up to the curb to let me out at the bank branch where Charlie's funds are deposited—money he's stolen from the Russian Mafia drug lords.

As I venture through the revolving doors of the four-story stone building, I wonder if I should tell Tom about my strange dream while I lay in a coma. I have not, I realize, simply because I am questioning what is reality. Is Arthur alive and I am asleep and dreaming again?

I keep thinking about what Jesus said: *We are all in God's dream.*

It was a stunning revelation. Changed everything—the way I formerly viewed life. I want to believe I am sane, but I wonder.

Tom has unwavering confidence in me that I can convince the bank manager to give me access to Charlie's bank account. I've memorized the account number and exactly what he wants me to say.

"Don't deviate from script," he cautions me.

I recall Tom telling me how he found out about Charlie's private account. He'd hacked Charlie's phone two months before and obtained the information required to close his Grand Cayman account. The money was going to a private banking group in Mexico City. It sounded to me like Tom intended to keep Charlie's stash.

I am pretty sure the money I deposited in the four other bank transfers would be given to the Central Intelligence Agency for use in their nefarious secretive tasks. It is the only way Tom can clear his name with the Agency. He is counting on the fact that Charlie has been discreet about his personal money transfers. And would not tell even if arrested. Ultimately, I have no choice but to trust Tom.

The bank manager's name is too difficult to pronounce, so I simply referred to him as Sir. "Sir, I need to close this account and transfer the funds to an account in Mexico City," I inform him.

He accesses his computer to find the account.

I wait, not so patiently, wondering what to do if something goes terribly wrong. Like he alerts the police to my illegal activity.

"I do not see your name on the account, Miss Daniels," Francisco Somebody reports. His dark gaze is incriminating.

"If you will check the original application," I tell him, "you will discover that I co-signed with Mr. Darby when he opened the account in 1991." Tom made sure I repeated that script twice.

Francisco performs an archive search using the account number.

"Yes, I see it. Daphanie Daniels." He looks up at me, smiling. "Credentials, please." His large hand extends my way.

I hand him my Washington D.C. driver's license with an updated photo of me since I look like Tom's deceased wife. He also wants to see my passport. No problem. I pass it over the desk to him.

And wait. He takes a long time.

"Are we good?" I inquire.

He looks up, a question lingering in his expression.

"May I ask why Mr. Darby is not here with you?"

"He has a very important job, so he sent me."

"Can he be reached by phone to verify?"

"Not at this time. Perhaps I should come back another time."

"No, no, that is not necessary."

"Thank you. I know Charlie will be pleased."

The manager proceeds to transfer five-million, two-hundred thirty-four thousand Euros into a bank account at the designated bank in Mexico City. I am suspicious that my ruse has gone all too smoothly. I keep thinking that Tom and I have missed something.

Francisco's desk phone rings. "Yes. Fine."

I look at him. "Are we done? Do I get a receipt?"

"Of course." He prints me a copy. "Oh, your cab driver just phoned and said to tell you to exit the bank through the backdoor."

I think about the request.

"Miss Daniels, shall I show you the way out?"

"Yes, please."

We exit his office and enter a series of hallways that leads to the rear of the building. Up ahead is a door with a glass insert that invites in the bright afternoon sunlight. I wonder if Tom ran into trouble and that is why he is picking me up at the back of the bank.

As I exit the building, a man wearing a hoodie approaches me. I do not get a warm and fuzzy feeling about my situation. Tom and the cab I came in are nowhere to be seen. I've been tricked.

Then something cold pokes me.

"Keep walking, Dorothy. I have a pistol in your side."

Startled, I am speechless at first. Then, as we walk, I take a good look at my assaulter. "Agent Charlie Darby!"

"Yes, clever woman. You did my bidding and didn't know it."

"What do you mean?" He nudges me toward the black car.

"You think Thomas Kessler is smarter than me?"

Charlie shoves me in the passenger seat and handcuffs my wrists. I try to open the door after he slammed it, but it's locked.

Double S-S!

Charlie nonchalantly trots around the front of the car and fills the driver's seat, his smirk as big as Kansas. "Cat got your tongue?"

I am seething a slow burn. His devious grin irks me.

"First time I've ever known you to be speechless."

I despise this man. No, I hate him. *Jesus, forgive me!*

Charlie ignites the engine and locks his gaze on me.

"So you know, I left my personal account number in my pocket on purpose." He sadistically laughs. "I knew Tom would find it."

"Wait a minute? You set us up, so we would transfer the illegal Russian drug profits to new accounts?" My mind is whirling

"Yeah, couldn't do it without getting caught."

Double D-D! I want to clobber him.

"Plus, I didn't have *you* to do the bidding."

I wonder where Tom is—is he dead?

* * *

Tom is starting to worry. "Keep the motor going," he tells the cabbie. "I need to step inside the building and check something."

"Want me to go with you?" Kelly asks.

"No."

Once inside the bank, he approaches a teller. "A woman with blond hair—about my age—was just here. Did she speak with one of the managers?" He waits for the male employee to check.

"Miss Daphanie Daniels?"

"Yes. Who helped her?"

"Mr. Jacinski. Shall I buzz him?"

"Please do." Tom steps to the side of the counter and waits.

Five minutes later, a tall skinny man with thinning hair the color of mud appears in the doorway and motions Tom to come with him.

"I'm Francisco Jacinski. And you are?"

"A friend of Daphanie Daniels," Tom replies. "Is she still here with you?" They walk down a long hallway and enter an office.

"No, I showed Ms. Daniels to the back entrance, per request."

"Who requested it?" Tom realizes the situation has gone bongos.

"Why, the cab driver she came with," he replies.

"Did you see her get into a cab?"

"No. We parted at the door."

"Thank you, Mr. Jacinski."

"Is there a problem?" he calls after his visitor.

Tom keeps walking. Who made that call? Did Dorothy decide to run away—maybe take the next flight out of Hell for America?

Or was she tricked, possibly in police custody?

19

"**I WANTED TO TAKE** an ocean cruise around Grand Cayman," I inform CIA Agent Charlie Darby, "but certainly not with you."

"Lover boy does not deserve you, Dorothy."

"And you do, Charlie? Are you going to kill me?"

He laughs as the ocean breeze undoes every strand of hair I placed in order this morning to make myself presentable.

"No, but you are going to undo what you did for Tom."

"What does that mean?" A spray of water assaults my perfectly made-up face. The late afternoon is too warm so the wet feels good.

"We'll be visiting the locations where you transferred the drug money," he replies. "I hope you possess the information we'll need."

"I don't," I declare. "Tom never told me. And I wouldn't tell you even if I did know." What keeps me alive is the mystery.

Which means Tom does not totally trust me or he would've told me—not that I would remember, anyhow. I am caught between the struggle of two lesser-than-honest men after a boatload of money.

"Well, in that case, we'll need to phone Tom," Charlie says. "But not until we are in the air and well on our way to Mexico City."

I feel sick at my stomach, and it's not from the bumpy boat ride.

* * *

Back in Tennessee, Daniel Leon Mason has been transferred from the Miami, Florida facility to the Columbia, Tennessee county jail. Detective Galena Chico and Captain Marilyn Colbert are about to interrogate him. Hopefully, they will get a full confession to two homicides in exchange for a lighter sentence than Murder One.

The nephew of a former Russian drug lord who formerly directed Kentucky trafficking sits at a metal table, his wrists bound and feet chained. He looks pissed off. Galena takes the lead.

"Danny, I'm Detective Chico."

"I know who you are," he slurs, more from fatigue than his last hit of cocaine. "Better make my offer good, or I'm mute."

"We expected no less," Galena says. "We know you worked for Coffee Call and placed a deadly substance in Dorothy Powell's latte with intent to murder her." She names the date in early March.

"Too bad she didn't drink it," he harks.

He's a smart aleck. Galena is ready to slap him around a bit, show him who's in charge, but she won't show her true temperament until she has the information the police need. Specifically, was he also sent to Columbia to murder Zoey Jackson? So, who ordered the hit?

The interview continues another ten minutes with no results.

"I'll take over from here."

Captain Colbert lays out a scenario regarding how Danny can be placed in a safer prison than the country where he was apprehended. In exchange for signing a full confession to murdering Gloria Bolton and Zoey Jackson, he will receive a lesser sentence than the death penalty. Galena disapproves of coercing him to admit to Zoey's murder, reasoning he would take the deal and lie. But it isn't her call.

The interview goes on another twenty minutes before Mason signs on the dotted line. He is removed from the interview room, leaving Galena facing the captain. They stand glaring at one another.

"Do you think he's being truthful?" Marilyn asks.

"I think he's saving his butt, Captain. But at least we can put Gloria Bolton's and Zoey Jackson's unsolved cases to bed. And we can only hope his confession will give Gerry Bolton some closure."

"Grief takes a while." Marilyn wonders what Nancy-Drew Dorothy is up to—why she hasn't phoned to report her location. An undercover agent in France gave her an out, if she wants to take it.

*　*　*

All I see below our plane is miles and miles of ocean water. The last thing I wanted was to ride in a bumpy eight-seater private jet through the outskirts of a blithering hurricane. By now, Tom will realize I am off Hell's grid—not that I'm in any better position.

"Couldn't we just wait a day before flying to Mexico City?" I ask.

"I'm on a timetable, Dorothy," Charlie replies. "Sorry the bumps make you nauseous." His grin says he's enjoying my misery.

"Did you talk to Tom about my bank account?"

"He's tossed his burner, so I can't reach him."

"I know the number to his other emergency burner."

"Well, well, fancy that!" Charlie huffs. "What is it?"

"No, no!" I tsk tsk him with a finger. "Negotiations first."

"What do you want, Dorothy?"

"If I give you back your money, I want a safe flight home."

"Nashville, Tennessee."

"Yes."

"You'd give up your young lover so quickly?"

"He's used me just like you want to," I explain. "So yes."

"How do you know you can trust me?"

"I don't, Charlie. But I have one playing card left."

"What is it?"

"Tom doesn't know I'm giving him up. He'll come after me—to save me. It's in his nature. He did it twice before, so . . . a deal?"

"You want me to let you call Tom's emergency prepaid cell phone number and tell him where we are?" He glares at me.

"Yes. It's the only way to obtain his cooperation," I say. "Tom trusts me. I'll make the call—like you don't know I'm doing it—and he'll come running to save me." I am inventing an escape scenario.

"First you'll help me get my personal funds back," Charlie says.

I nod. "No problem."

"No tricks, Dorothy. Fully cooperate and I'll send you home on a plane while Tom comes to me like a child led by Jesus."

I don't like his analogy, but what can I expect from a criminal?

"Just so you know, my freedom does not depend on whether you have the ability to obtain the new account numbers of banks with the drug funds," I say. "I do my thing and I leave. Agreed?"

He nods.

Whoopee! I know Charlie is no match for Tom.

20

Tuesday, July 18

"LOOK, TOM. SHE'S not here," Kelly says, bone-weary from riding in the rental car. "We've searched every island so it's time to recognize Dorothy is gone. Either by her own volition or someone took her."

Kelly knew that Charlie had kidnapped the bothersome woman. He'd promised to pay her a percent of his stash if she helped him recoup his retirement. In a way, she was fulfilling a double-agent role.

Tom is not pleased at the idea, but she's possibly right.

"What do you want to do?" Kelly asks. "We can't wander around the islands indefinitely hoping she'll show up."

"I know, but I'm not going back to D.C. with you until I know Dorothy is safe. I got her into this trouble and we're getting her out."

He glares at Kelly. Did she have something to do with this?

"Who did you call on the phone?" he inquires.

"When?" Kelly turquoise eyes roll as her thick black eyebrows arch. "Oh, no, you're not blaming this on me."

Tom spins the rental car around in the middle of a winding mountain road and heads back to their hotel to check out. Time to depart Hell and search elsewhere. "Yesterday. . ."

"Was a tough day for you, Tom. I get it."

"When we were in the cab waiting for Dorothy to come out of the bank, who did you call? Better that you tell me the truth."

"My mother." Kelly laughs. "She worries about me."

"With good reason. Give me your phone."

"What?" Kelly slinks back against the passenger door.

"I need to know you didn't do something bad."

"Betray you? No. I like you, Tom."

"But you don't like Dorothy. I see it every time you look at her. I can't imagine you are jealous of an eighty-three-year-old woman."

Kelly huffs then sadistically laughs. "Yet, you dig her."

"Yes, I dig her. And I'll dig your grave if I find out you're lying to me. I want the money in Mexico City. So that's where we'll go."

Kelly knew better than to argue. She rode the rest of the way to the Kimton Seafire Resort and Spa and packed up like a good little girl. Tom paid the tab and they drove straight to the airport.

Boarding was a nightmare—it appeared all the tourists on three islands had decided to get out of Dodge. Or Hell.

* * *

Charlie checks us into the Hotel Historico Central Hotel in downtown Mexico City. My head is dizzy from hop-skipping across the world in search of fortune. Arthur would roll over in the dust of his ashes if he could witness this phenomenon. I think some creature from outer space has captured my mind, body, and soul then sent me to a form of Hell I will never escape. God, help me survive today!

I had seen pictures of Mexico City in books I checked out of the public library when I was still engaged in teaching high school students. But actually, being in the city is another whole thing. I wish Tom were here with me instead of the insidious Agent Darby.

I should have known when I visited the CIA headquarters in D.C. and Charlie greeted me so kindly that something was amiss. I let him take my little black book into the Director's office, copy the account numbers recorded there, without a smidgen of suspicion.

Then Gerry Bolton pointed out my error. Charlie had used the camera in his cell phone to copy the book. So, here I am. In this mess. All because of my stupidity. Who will rescue me now?

"I see that devious mind working, Dorothy. Care to elaborate?"

"On your grave," I sneer as we enter an elevator.

He laughs. "Do as you're told and I promise to send you home unharmed." He winks at me. I know he's kidding. I know too much to be turned loose to report his illegal activities. I'm as good as dead if I don't escape his clutches. And Tom has no idea where I am.

* * *

"What makes you think Dorothy is in Mexico City?" Kelly inquires as she buckles her seatbelt in anticipation of the jet's liftoff.

"You told Charlie about the money transfer—only thing that makes sense." He probes her face for an indication he's right.

"Dorothy/Daphanie could've bought a ticket to America," Kelly says for argument's sake. If Tom finds out she helped Charlie . . .

"Dorothy loves me, Kelly. She won't admit it because she's scared. She was a former biology teacher, not used to clandestine activities. She would never betray me. Maybe you would."

Kelly snickers as the plane shoots nearly straight up in the air.

"You think that's funny?" Tom glances down at the island falling away like a camera zooming out. Clouds then engulf the plane.

"What are you doing with all the money Dorothy/Daphanie transferred to new accounts?" Kelly asks. "Are you going to give it back to the Russian mob, turn it in to the CIA, or keep it?"

"I already took care of it." He glanced over at the young agent who is still having trouble wiping her—he won't go there even in his wicked thoughts. "It's not your problem, Kelly. Let it go."

Bruised from being dressed down, she leans back and closes her eyes, more tired than she realized. Next thing she knows, sleep captures her. When her breathing evens out, Tom makes a call.

"Director Carlton," he tells the receptionist.

He waits only a few seconds before the call transfers.

"Jack here, Tom! Good to hear from you."

"I have to make this conversation quick."

"We got your text message with the new account numbers. The Agency owes you big for capturing these drug funds and returning them to us. We've spent decades looking. How's our girl doing?"

"Our girl is missing." Tom watches Kelly to make sure she's not pretending to sleep and memorizing his every word over the phone.

"Where are you and when did that happen?"

"I'm inflight to Mexico City," Tom reveals. "Dorothy never returned after transferring Charlie's funds to a new account." He would not blame his seatmate until he was sure she betrayed him.

"Send me a full report when you can," the Director orders. "Her daughter has been calling our office and is worried sick."

"I hope you've said nothing about what we're doing."

"Mums the word." The phone connection crackles.

Tom unbuckles his seatbelt and slips down the aisle of the plane to the back to use the john. Kelly is not trustworthy. At some point he needs to dump her. She called Charlie while they were in the cab waiting for Dorothy to come out of the bank. It was the only thing that made sense. She despised her alcoholic mom.

"You still there, Tom?" the Director asks.

"Yes, I presume you know Drop-Dead-Gorgeous is with me."

"We sent her to Paris to find you, but no, I didn't know she'd joined forces with you and Dorothy," Jack reveals. "I sent someone to bring Dorothy home. Did she tell you?" He waits.

"No, who?" Dorothy doesn't trust him. This proves it.

"Agent Jim Grossman. He approached her in Paris at the park but she flat turned him down." Jack laughs. "I think she likes you."

"Not enough to tell me, though," Tom quips, a bit angry.

"You and Kelly come on home. I'll have my international guys look for the missing Dorothy. She must be weary at her age."

Tom doesn't think age enters into the equation. Dorothy is smart, and if Charlie has her, she will find a way to cut him loose.

"Signing off. I'm staying off the grid for now."

* * *

I stand outside the hotel on the sidewalk thinking the historical relic in downtown Mexico reminds me of a Starbuck's or a bookstore. But packaging can be deceiving. I recall the first time I saw Clint Howard. He was bigger than life. So gorgeously handsome. And I was so lonely with Arthur thrown to the wind the year before.

The CIA agent befriended her and made innuendos that he was more than just interested in keeping company with her. In fact, she could've slept with him within a month had she a mind to do so. But being a Christian meant something to her. God did not honor sexual relationships outside of holy matrimony. The Bible clearly states that a man and woman are to leave their parents and become as one in body and spirit. Now, it seems that Tom is ready to marry her.

Should I accept his proposal when we next meet?

"What are you doing, Dorothy? Just standing there?"

"You wouldn't understand if I told you, Charlie. My thoughts are higher than your thoughts; my ways higher than yours." I recall what God had said to one of the ancient men of the Old Testament.

"That sounds biblical." Charlie grasps me by the arm. "Shall we go to supper? We haven't eaten since breakfast and I'm hungry."

21

THE SUN SETS IN Mexico City just after 8 p.m. during summers. The temperature only reached 70 degrees Fahrenheit at lunchtime today, so I am wearing a sweater as the air is quickly cooling down. Charlie tells me it can be 50 degrees mid-nights in July. I believe him, if nothing else as we ride in a city cab to a local restaurant.

I note how the houses on the hillsides looks like colored stacked blocks. From my recall of geography, Mexico City is boxed in by two mountain ranges. To the west are the Sierra Occidentals. To the east, the Sierra Madre Oriental. I'm impressed with my recall and wonder if jet-setting around the world has boosted my mental faculties.

I sure don't want Dementia or Alzheimer's to attack me while I'm having fun. "Where are we going to dine?" I ask my date.

"The Rosa Negra," he replies. "It's one of the top recommended restaurants in the city. Google says you can get anything from lobster to crabcakes. I hear their Baked Alaska is to die for." He snickers.

"That was not necessary," I chasten him.

"Also, a slice of Apple Pie al a mode will tempt you." He glares at me a moment. "Have I offended you in some way, Dorothy?"

"Your very presence offends me," I am boldly honest.

"Aren't you hungry? Don't wound the hand that feeds you."

"Aren't you full of platitudes! You stole my appetite when you kidnapped me." The cab pulls up to the front of the restaurant.

"Get out! We're going in and playing nice."

No comment, I follow like a long-lost sheep. We enter a foyer with very tall ceilings. The color scheme is blood-red and brown.

Charlie tells the woman at the counter we have a reservation.

We enter the restaurant proper and I spy large rectangular planks suspended from ceiling beams with yellow lighting. Tables covered in white-linen cloths match the seat covers of metal chairs. The restaurant is spacious and quaint and I suspect the food is expensive.

"You like?" he asks as a server seats me.

A lot, but don't say. The food odors wafting the airways are to die for—I immediately regret my thoughts. Now seated, I snap a cloth napkin and spread it out in my lap. Our Mexican waiter, Johnny-on-the-spot, delivers a glass jug of cold water with a platter of hot bread. I speak a little Spanish, but not enough to read the menu and know exactly what I am ordering. Charlie is much better at it.

"Do you see anything on the menu you want?" he inquires.

"Why don't you order for the both of us," I suggest.

"Okay. Let's start with the crabcakes and end up with apple pie for dessert." He closes the laminated menu and glares at me.

"What's in-between? Our entrée?"

"Lobster—might be our last meal."

"You mean yours. I intend to survive."

"I like your savvy, Dorothy. No wonder Tom took a liking to you. He tells me you are in your eighties, but you don't look at it."

"Thanks to Dr. Sharra. He lifted my face."

Charlie snickers as our server inquires what we want to drink. Water is fine for me. But when Charlie orders two glasses of white wine I don't protest. I'll need to relax a bit if I get a wink of sleep tonight. He wants to talk about what Tom and I have been doing.

I don't. Rather I ask questions about Mexico City.

The service I am soon to learn is superb. And I will go away with my stomach satisfied. I eat heartily, reminded of what Charlie said. This might be our last meal before the police catch and arrest us.

* * *

Back in Tennessee, Lorene is about to lock up the house for the evening and enjoy some leftover pizza with a movie when her front doorbell rings. "Goodness! Graham must've forgotten something."

She rushes to the foyer and peeks through the side glass of the front door to see who's calling at this late hour in the day.

It's someone with a large plant, their face hidden by the flowers. The doorbell continues to ring. It's not her birthday, so what is this all about? She unlocks the door. "May I help you?" she asks.

"Floral delivery for Lorene Perkins," the young man replies. "Is she here? Specific instructions say I give them only to her."

"I'm her, uh, Lorene. Who sent the plant?" It has rather large leaves with huge flaming-red flowers. "Are you sure this is for me?"

"Yep, from the International Florist Delivery."

"Okay then, I'll take the plant. Thank you."

He leaves and Lorene sets the plant on the foyer floor and plucks the card from its holder. It is signed, *From an overseas friend.*

After locking the door, Lorene trots to the kitchen to get her cell phone to call Claire Burkes. "Your mother sent me flowers."

"What? From where?"

"I don't know," Lorene replies. "It's a strange plant."

"And it's a clue," Claire says. We need to take the plant to a botany specialist and find out where it grows," she decides.

"Are you sure?"

"Yes. I'll be at your house in the morning by eight o'clock."

"If Dorothy needs our help, should I alert Detective Chico?"

"No, not yet. Let's find out where the plant grows first then we'll both go and see her," Claire declares. "Thank you, Lorene."

"No, thank your clever mother."

"Who has a knack for getting into trouble."

* * *

"You don't trust me to sleep alone?" I glare at evil-eyed Charlie. "You can leave the door open between our rooms."

"Not an option. You'll get one of the queen beds." He checks out the window overlooking the parking lot then closes the curtains.

I stand there, frustrated at the situation.

"You can take your shower first and get ready for bed."

"I don't have any pajamas," I remind him. "Or a toothbrush."

"Look in the paper sack. I bought you PJs from the gift shop at the airport," he says. "Size 10, right? I'll have your clothes cleaned overnight so you'll be fresh tomorrow when you visit the bank."

"What about my toothbrush?"

"A guest packet of toiletries is provided by the hotel."

"I'm not sleepy yet. I slept too much on the plane."

He snickers. "It was only two Benadryl, Dorothy."

"I want to see the 10:00 news," I insist.

"It's in Spanish—won't do you much good."

"It's illegal to kidnap an American citizen," I protest.

"You were already kidnapped. I just took over the role."

"Smarty pants! I bet you gave your teachers hell."

"Was I smarter than them? You bet. Teachers just couldn't keep up with me," he brags while unbuttoning his shirt. His chest is a maze of blond fuzz but there are four scars from bullet holes.

"Go take your turn in the bathroom, Dorothy."

I grab the sack with my PJ's and slump into the bathroom. I am travel-weary. This is not my idea of a vacation anymore.

"Don't lock the door, or I'll kick it down!" he calls out.

"I'm not worried about you looking—I've nothing worth the trouble." I laugh, but there are tears clouding my vision.

I can only pray that Lorene got my Ruby Slippers. It's a native plant found in Grand Cayman Isles. A Dwarf Oakleaf Hydrangea. While Tom was in the restroom in the foyer where tickets are purchased to view the botanical gardens, I bought the plant and sent it to Lorene. She'll call Claire and they'll figure out I was in Hell.

But how long will it take them to find me in Mexico City?

22

Wednesday, July 19

CHARLIE AND I WERE seated in Hotel Historico Central's restaurant enjoying breakfast. Surprisingly, our room only costs $130 a night American currency. He didn't book it again for tonight—which made me question where I would be. Dead or . . . "What?"

"I see that tricky mind of yours working."

"You know, Charlie, Tom is trained to track down people," I tell my date while I savor my second cup of Java coffee. Mexican chefs know how to create a café mocha latte better than I've had at Columbia's version of Coffee Call. They use a special type of cocoa bean that is strong and, when mixed with milk and sugar, is delicious.

"No worries, by the time he gets here we'll be gone."

"My home, right? You promised if I cooperate."

"Depends on whether you are a good girl or not."

"How old are you, Charlie?" He's a seasoned agent; I guestimate he's in his late fifties. "You had a fling with Daphanie, didn't you?"

Let's probe his psyche and see where it leads.

"I tried, but she turned me down flat."

"You must've been in your thirties when you worked with her—stealing secrets from the Americans," I continue my assessment of his attempt to woo the lovely Daphanie, a little older and wiser.

"I don't want to talk about that." His gaze roams the room.

"It must've gotten your goose good when she fell in love with Tom and turned on you and your Russian thugs." I am on a roll.

"This conversation ends now!" He bangs the tabletop.

I only smile. "What did you do for revenge?"

"I reported her to the SVR but they didn't believe me. What proof did I have?" He splays his hands. "Then she married him."

I chuckle. "Tom gets under your skin, yet you've worked with him for decades. Why? You could have had Mark Hagen kill him."

"Where is the fun in that? I want him to suffer."

I wonder how far I can push this without serious retaliation? What if I stand up and just scream, "Help! He's kidnapped me!"

The irritation in Charlie's expression takes the cake.

His silence is even scarier than his outrage. I'm done needling him. We sit for a moment, glaring hard at one another. *A Mexican standoff,* I think, then cannot help but smile. "You okay, Charlie?"

"We should go. Bank opens at nine. You know what to do."

"Yeah, I know." I retrieve my lipstick from my purse and proceed to smear my lips with bright red. "What?"

"They tell me putting on lipstick without a mirror is a southern-girl thing," he comments. "You didn't miss a lick."

"I've missed a lot of licks in the past, but I'm more in tune with myself than I've ever been," I tell him. "Watch out, Charlie!"

"You think you're going to cross me?"

"Just a fair warning—even though this is not love or war."

We take the metro to Banco de Mexico 6 Avenue 5 de Mayo 2. Not that the name means anything to me, but that is where Charlie's retirement stash rests for the moment. The rat in Hell betrayed me and gave Charlie the account number where I routed his funds.

We walk into the bank together. He's like glue to my back and I want to scream—which gives me an idea. I can fake a physical attack of some kind. The teller will alert a medic and I'll be swept off to a hospital. What can Charlie do to stop me? Nothing, I think.

"Go on, Dorothy. Delay is not in your favor."

"So, you say. . ." I march up to the counter and make eye contact with the teller. "Do you speak *ingles*?" I know some Spanish.

He smiles. "I do. How may I help you this morning?"

"I need to transfer funds." I grab my chest like I'm in pain.

"Credentials, please."

Doesn't he see I have a health problem?

I remove my Daphanie Daniels' driver's license and give it to him," grabbing my chest again and coughing profusely.

"Are you sick, Miss Daniels? Were you tested for Covid?"

I wave him off. "No Covid, but may I have some water?"

"Perhaps you need to sit down." He motions for the guard.

I notice Charlie walking toward me. This is where my theater experience in high school will really pay off. I let go of myself and slink to the floor, eyes shut tightly and purposely struggling for my breath. Immediately, I feel two cool hands on my arms.

"She's with me," Charlie says.

"We can call a doctor," the guard says.

"No, Mama has these spells."

I feel a prick in my arm. Then everything goes black.

* * *

It's 9:35 a.m. when Tom and Kelly are standing outside the Banco de Mexico branch where Charlie's funds were transferred.

"You think they're already inside the bank?" she asks.

"Yeah, doors opened for business at nine."

"You might be wrong about them coming here," she says.

"I'm not. Charlie wants his retirement secured. He needs Dorothy's help." Tom peers through the plate-glass window.

"Are we going inside unannounced to face off with them? That is, if they are actually in there and we didn't fly here for nothing."

"I came for Dorothy. I don't know why you came."

"For this." Kelly points at 9 mm pistol at Tom.

"What did that sleaze bag promise you?"

"Enough money to look for another less dangerous job," she replies. "Walk away, Tom. I won't hesitate to shoot."

"Not on your life." He spies two medics coming out the side door of the bank carrying a stretcher. Charlie Darby is behind them.

"If he hurt Dorothy, I swear . . ."

"Better worry more about if I hurt you, Tom."

"Give me that thing!" He jerks the pistol out of her hand.

23

I AM AT ARTHUR'S memorial service. I'm fast learning that time is playing a trick on me. Is this the past, present, or future?"

I glance around and see so many of our friends. Coming through the backdoor is Detective Butch and his cute secretary Ellie. A young woman I recognize is with them. Zoey Jackson.

She's still breathing. This is years before she will die.

Brother Kenny, my Methodist minister, is standing on the stage, preparing to address the assembly—people who respected and honored Arthur. I want to scream, THIS ISN'T REAL!

I've done all this before. Perhaps I am only dreaming.

Lorene stands behind me as the service ends. She is weeping.

"I need to talk to Lorene before I leave," I whisper to Claire.

"Are you sure, Mama?"

I nod. "Go on back to the house. Food will be coming."

I catch my friend as she exits the door to the funeral home. "Can we go get a coffee somewhere?" I ask. "It's important."

Lorene nods, teary-eyed because not only is Arthur deceased, Crawford had bit the bullet by now—so to speak.

"I thought you'd want to be with Claire—after, you know."

"I can't do anything for Arthur now, but there are things you need to know, for your own protection."

She follows me outdoors and we get in my Cadillac.

"You're not even crying, Dorothy. Are you okay?"

I start the engine. "I know you don't believe in prophetic dreams, but I do. Crawford did not die of natural causes."

"You're scaring me, Dorothy. Are you okay?"

"Listen to me, Lorene! Crawford was scared to death."

Lorene only shakes her head.

"I'm not making this up, Lorene. It's already happened."

"You're not thinking straight, you need to go home and rest."

"I will, but not until we have a frank discussion and you know exactly what to expect. Do you know your daughter Heather has breast cancer?" She lives in Kentucky, so Lorene rarely sees her.

"That's mean, Dorothy. Don't say stuff like that."

"Why? Because it might come true?"

I am tired of pussyfooting around with people that say they love me. If I can change anything, save anybody, I will.

"I don't want any coffee," Lorene says.

She's peeved at me because of what I said about Heather.

"I'm only sharing information for your own good," I say.

"Take me back to the funeral home right now."

"I know you're mad at me and I am so sorry."

"Why aren't you grieving for Arthur?"

"I am, in my own way—it's just I see things from a different perspective." I know that makes little sense to Lorene.

"I am still sick to my stomach that Crawford has passed!" She sucks in a breath. "Soon, I'll need to pack up all of his clothes and the things that were important to him and give them away."

"I know, but I help you."

She frowns. "You say that like it's already happened."

"It has. Once. What I am trying to do is prevent everything else bad coming in the future." Our gazes are loaded and locked.

"You want to change Fate?" Lorene utters. "Is that possible?"

"I don't know. If I can't, Clyde Willems will soon die, too. In time, Lloyd Peters will be shot in his apartment and burnt to a crisp during a fire. Zoey Jackson will be murdered and folks will believe she committed suicide. We'll have a new friend move here, Alicia."

Lorene looks at me like I'm totally off my rocker.

"I know all of this sounds crazy, but it's true. I am going to fall in love with a CIA agent posing as Clint Howard. He'll come to Columbia to manage the Senior Citizen Center. And a high school rival of mine, Gloria Bolton, will be poisoned by a latte meant for me." I am so on a roll. "I'll be targeted by a hitman. Mark Hagen."

Lorene is shaking her head.

"What?"

"I've always said you have a big imagination, and that you should write a novel. It will definitely be a best-seller," she mouths.

"You don't believe me." I sigh. At least, I've tried.

* * *

Dorothy is still out like a light switched off since Charlie Darby shot her up with a strong sedative. But paramedics speaking fluent Spanish had insisted a doctor check her out in the hospital ER.

He was this moment arguing with the physician on call. "My mother has a health problem. She faints. I have meds for her."

"Until she's thoroughly examined, we can't release her."

"She also has dementia—which makes her fantasize about unimaginable scenarios. She may tell you the craziest stories if she wakes up in one of your patient rooms," Charlie warns the doctor.

"Let me do my job, Mr. Darby. Then we'll release your mother into your care." He stares at the American. "*Si*."

It isn't the way Charlie envisioned their bank experience. All Dorothy had to do was transfer the money then go home.

But, then, she did not trust anyone. Fear for her life made her do something stupid. Now he'd have to play out his own fantasy and hope to hell it worked. Getting arrested would not go well for him.

"Check her out. I'll wait to hear from you."

* * *

Tom is in the process of questioning the teller that assisted Daphanie Daniels at the counter. "She suddenly started acting weird and swaying like she had vertigo. An American came to her rescue."

"Could you describe the American?" Tom asked.

"A man. He said he was her son."

"Did someone call for medical assistance?" Tom already knew Dorothy was taken away in a med van. "Where was she taken?"

"I already told the police all I know."

All of this conversation was in Spanish—which fortunately Tom knew well from his CIA training. "Which hospital?"

"Why do you want to know? Who are you?"

Tom produces his CIA creds and the young teller nods. Her cooperation is stellar. He listens carefully to the man's description and determines the American is indeed Charlie Darby.

"Where did the paramedics take Ms. Daniels?"

"One of the hospitals."

"Which one?" Tom demands.

"I'm not sure."

"Take a guess."

Tom memorized the address and returned to the rental car where Kelly was restlessly waiting. One of her hands is strapped to the steering wheel. "What did you find out?" she utters.

"Dorothy's been taken to a local hospital to be checked out," he tells Kelly as he removes her shackles then ignites the engine to exit the parking lot. Silence fills the car while they drive to the address.

* * *

Nurse Carla is attending the older woman. Blood tests had been run and it appears Ms. Daniels had overdosed on sleeping pills.

"Oh . . ." I groan, feeling I'm on a Ferris Wheel doing loops. I am reminded of the time Arthur and I went to the Memphis County Fair and rode every crazy ride for twenty cents each. That was when we were young and foolish and didn't mind upchucking our hotdogs.

"She's coming to," Carla tells her companion to get the doctor.

"Oh, dear God, I have an awful headache." I sit up and look around. "Where am I? Where is my friend, Lorene?"

"Don't try to get up, Ms. Daniels, you might fall."

"Where am I?" I try to focus my bleary eyes.

"Mexico City, in a hospital," Carla replies.

I drop my head on the pillow. The terror is back.

"I'll get your son," she says.

"Lance? No, my son is dead." I grab hold of the nurse. "The man claiming to be my son abducted me. He's CIA and dirty."

I can see she does not believe me.

"I'm telling the truth."

Coming through the door is a middle-aged Mexican doctor. His light skin advises me that he has English blood intermingled with Spanish genes. He has a bulging tummy but appears to be joyful.

"Ah . . . our patient is finally awake. How do you feel?"

"Like an atomic bomb has been dropped on me," I answer.

He smiles. The son has warned him that his mother has dementia and invents scenarios. "You'll feel much better very soon. How about a strong cup of pilon coffee? It will counteract the pills."

"What pills?" I sit up, struggling for more clarity.

"The sleeping pills you took. They had a latent effect."

"I took no sleeping pills." I point to the door. "That maniac that was with me is a CIA agent. He kidnapped me. Call the police and have him arrested. I want to go home. RIGHT NOW!"

My emotions are all over the place. Did I transfer the money from the bank? I try to recall exactly what happened, but could not.

"I'll get her son," Carla offers.

"No, don't! He's dangerous. Call my friend, Tom." I rattle off a burner number I memorized before I was removed from Hell.

24

UNFORTUNATELY, A TRAFFIC accident had delayed Tom and Kelly from getting to the hospital ER in a timely manner. By the time they arrived, Daphanie Daniels had been dismissed. A doctor reported an American claiming to be her son checked her out. No leads, for now.

They were back in the rental again. "We should go back to the bank and talk to the manager," Kelly suggests. "If Dorothy fainted before she performed the deed, Charlie will not leave Mexico."

"You're right. He needs his retirement stash." Tom removed his phone to make a phone call. It rings several times.

"Who are you calling?" Kelly wonders.

Tom holds up a finger. *Don't talk.*

Kelly listens to the one-sided conversation, not yielding much information that is helpful to her. In time, given the opportunity, she will call Charlie and check in. Hopefully, he has his money.

"Okay," Tom says, "I'll text you the address." He listens to the person at the other end of the call. "Fine. Have your men check."

Then ends the call and locks his gaze on Kelly.

"Check what?" she inquires, hands tied in front of her.

Tom ignites the engine. "Are you hungry?"

"You want to eat? What about our business at the bank?"

"Taken care of," he says and they drive out of the hospital parking lot. There is no more he can do for Dorothy.

* * *

"I don't think this is a good idea, Charlie." Dorothy feels a nudge at her back. The pistol. I won't make another scene.

"Do your good diligence and get me my money. You know the account number. I'm not a very patient man."

Another nudge as they enter the same bank again. I approach the same teller. She immediately recognizes me. "Good afternoon."

"Ms. Daniels? Are you feeling better?" she asks from behind an enclosed glassed-in counter. Her gaze skitters to the son.

I glance back. Charlie is grinning. The cad.

"Much better, thank you for asking. A seizure of some sort."

"What can I do for you this afternoon?"

Dorothy hands her the bank account number. "I want you to close this account and have the money routed to this location."

"I'll need to see your creds again."

Another nudge at my back.

"No problem." Dorothy hands them over.

Fifteen minutes later, we are exiting the Banco de Mexico. In front of us are three police cars parked nose-parked to the curb.

"What's going on?" I ask Charlie, his pistol still in my side.

"Just keep walking like it has nothing to do with us."

I won't contest his decision and chance a lethal bullet.

"Hold it there! Both of you!" a gray-haired man steps from behind one of the squad cars. His gun is pointed at Agent Charlie.

Has the calvary arrived?

I actually snicker.

Charlie drops the gun and raises his hands.

"You're free to go, Ms. Powell," Director Carlton tells me. "You, Charlie," he sneers, "you're coming with us."

"How did you find me?" Charlie gives me a dirty look.

I feel like a kid let out of school and stick my tongue out at him. "Everybody gets what's coming to them. Bible rule #1."

The flurry of activity around me is stunning. I stand there like a knot on a log—as my deceased mother used to say. Then the squad cars back out and zoom away. I am left on the street, entirely alone.

Alone. It seems like that is always my fate.

I have no cash or credit cards to even purchase a bottle of water as I walk twenty blocks to the American Embassy. I explain my situation and a kind woman makes a call to my daughter, Claire.

"Hi. I'm in Mexico City. Book me an airline ticket home?"

"Mama! I thought you were in Hell."

"This was much worse."

"You sound winded. Are you sure you are okay?"

"I will be, Claire, given time."

"Are you alone?"

"Explaining my situation will take too long, Claire."

"Just tell me, did Thomas Kessler kidnap you?"

"Yes, but I encountered several other problems."

"Are you with him now?"

"Goodness, Claire, can your questions wait till I get home?"

"Tell me one thing, did you marry Tom?"

"Of course not, I'm old enough to be his mother."

But truth be known, I would've loved if this story had turned out with a happier ending. Me and Tom—riding off into the sunset. Roy Rogers and the woman he saved from a boring life.

"Okay, I'll book you a ticket home," Claire says.

"Thank you," I tell the U.S. representative as I hand her phone back. I'll just sit down and wait for my circumstances to change.

Claire's call comes in thirty minutes. The Embassy has me driven to the airport where my Daphanie Daniels' creds work to get me onboard a plane to Miami, Florida. From there, I'll fly to Nashville.

25

Thursday, July 20

I WAKE UP IN Claire's guest bedroom. My eyes bumpily fly open like the jet that landed in Nashville late last night. I hear familiar noises. June, screeching to the top of her lungs as her grandfather tickles her. Pounding sounds on the wood den floor—Billy jumping up and down while waiting his turn with Ted. At least my daughter and her husband are still together. Claire, laughing hard at the scene.

I'm the mother-in-law, so not my place to ask questions. I don't want to be a bother so I take a shower and dress for the day.

Tomorrow is Friday and I intend to secure my place at the Canasta table at the Senior Citizen Center in Columbia. Clint Howard won't be there; I know for sure. Agent Tom is still a mystery to me.

I scrub my head in the shower till it feels like my hair is going to fall out. I've lost ten pounds according to Claire's bathroom scales. I find the hair dryer in the cabinet then borrow her hairbrush.

The dryer sings loudly, but I don't care. I am finally home. Charlie Darby is under arrest. Drop-dead-gorgeous is probably on the other side of the world performing some nefarious tasks for the CIA. I wonder what Tom is up to. Did he keep all the money I transferred for Daphanie Daniels? It's none of my business anymore.

What about my feelings for him? Can I ignore them, too?

A knock comes at the bathroom door. I swipe the steam from the mirror and dare to look at my uplifted face. The knock persists.

I saunter over to the door, a towel draped around my naked body, and crack the space between me and Claire. "What?"

"Just wanted to make sure you are all right."

"Why wouldn't I be?" I shut the door and lock it. Then slide down the wall and let all hell break loose as I scream to the top of my lungs. Like lightning igniting thunder, the sounds are haunting.

* * *

Tom is in the Director's office in D.C. They are discussing the stolen Russian Mafia funds Charlie accumulated over the decades.

Drop-Dead Gorgeous

"You could've just kept it all," Jack tells Tom.
"I know. It didn't feel right. Did you pay Dorothy?"
"You were serious about putting her on the CIA payroll?"
"Damn straight I was!"
"Okay. I'll have a check cut and sent to her address."
"She doesn't have an address. She's homeless."
"Why don't you deliver it. Your chance to say goodbye."

Tom nods, unsure if he's ready to disconnect. Around Dorothy is like keeping company with a hurricane. You never know which way the storm will blow. And she's beautiful, charming, funny . . .

"Tom!" Jack snaps his fingers. "Earth is calling."

He shrugs.

"What are you thinking?"

"I don't know if her seeing me again is a good idea." Tom is embarrassed for tricking her into serving the CIA's purposes."

She might be mad enough to put a bullet between his eyes.

"What about the daughter's address?"

"No, I'll personally deliver the payment."

* * *

I did not call Lorene and warn her I was back. I wanted to see the surprise registered on her face. I wait, then ring the bell again.

Graham opens the door.

"Ms. Powell?"

"Yeah, I'm back. Is Lorene here?"

"No, she went to the Senior Citizen Center," he tells me. "They're having a junk sale to raise money for the local orphanage."

"Okay, thanks. I go over there and find her."

It feels good to be driving my own Audi, no handcuffs and fully in charge of my own destiny. Nobody is going to tell me what to do today. I'm footloose and free. Nobody is coming to arrest me for illegally posing as Daphanie Daniels. The July day is hot and bright.

And I am strangely optimistic about my future.

I cannot believe all the cars parked out in front of the Center. I spy Lorene's putrid-green Tesla, which confirms she's inside. I have to park a block away and walk to the Center, realizing I'm pretty tired from jet-setting around the world. But, at least, I am home now.

I see my friend on the other side of the large dining room. She is surrounded by our card buddies, Lizzy Hinson and Jane Murphy. There's another woman in their group I do not recognize.

My replacement at the Canasta card table!

Double D-D! I silently curse to myself.

I don't know what happened so suddenly but the quiet in the large hall stuns me for a second. Fingers are pointed at me. Eyes roam over me like I'm a space alien. Then everyone starts clapping.

For me.

"Oh, Dorothy!" Lorene grabs me and hugs me like I'm her long-lost relative she thought was dead but came back from the grave.

I am speechless. Everyone is gathering around me, asking so many questions about where I've been and what I've been doing. Feeling a bit claustrophobic, I push my way through my attentive audience and race for the door. Is this a panic attack? Or what?

PTSD? Even that thought frightens me.

26

I AM SEATED IN knee-high grass in the field where Arthur kept his cattle. It seems the only place I fit today after the rollercoaster ride I've had with Thomas Kessler. I'm still homeless and lonely.

"Lord, what are you going to do with me? I am an old woman with dreams that half came true and half nearly got me killed."

I feel a presence behind me and glance back.

"I thought I'd find you here."

He sits down in the grass beside me. I can smell his cologne. His hair is fresh-washed and he's clean-shaven. As handsome as a star on the big screen. "Why did you come, Tom?" I quietly ask.

"I thought you needed closure."

"From you?"

"From all of it. I'm sorry I got you involved."

I just sit there, thinking about what he's said.

"Do you have questions?"

"What happened to the money I transferred?"

"Gave it all back to the CIA."

"Even Charlie's retirement stash?"

He looks up at the clear-blue sky, deepening as the day wanes.

"I thought you would," I tell him. "You're a good person."

He grins then laughs; his arms folded around his knees as he longingly looks at me. "I'm going to miss you, Dorothy!"

I know I will miss him. But all good things come to an end.

"Was it all a game, Tom?" I inquire. "Was any of *us* real?"

"At first, yeah, but now I genuinely care for you."

"Because I look like Daphanie." I nod. "But, I'm not her."

"A good copy, though." He reaches over to grasp my cold hand.

A brisk breeze stirs the tall grassy field, yellow and ripe for the coming harvest in August. "What are you going to do now?"

"I need to finish out the year with the CIA, then I'll decide if I'm retiring," he tells me as the sun slips lower over the rolling green hills.

"It's beautiful here in Middle Tennessee," he comments.

"I wouldn't live any place else."

He nods, looking a little sad at saying goodbye.

I realize our nods mean as much as our language. I want to tell him I love him. I want to say I'll marry him. But all of this—this fantasy life—is something I need to put to bed. *Forever.*

"I brought you something." He reaches in his pants pocket.

Dear God, if it's a ring how can I say no?

He hands me an envelope. "What's this?"

"Open it. A surprise from the CIA."

The check to me is for $25,000. Director Carlton signed it. At the bottom it reads: For services rendered.

I nod again, no words to express my surprise.

"Well, I should go now."

He gets up and brushes the loose grass off his beige slacks. His shirt is a shade green, a contrast to his glistening brown eyes. The odor of him diminishes as he steps away from me.

"See you later, Dorothy."

I nod. I don't look back. No words to say goodbye.

27

Friday, November 24

AUTUMN HAS OUTSHINED every other season this year. Never were the reds and purples and golds so radiant against the green foliage changing to brown. I purchased a condo in Columbia against my daughter's wishes that I be planted near her as I grow older. While I can still walk, think, and talk, I prefer to be on my own around my friends and not dependent on Claire taking care of me.

Yesterday, our extensive family gathered at Claire's house for our Thanksgiving meal. I was no longer the center of attention, thank God! June assumed the spotlight with her new adventure as a student in the first grade. I sat most of the afternoon in a chair tucked behind the sofa, observing each precious soul that originally came from our union. *Me and Arthur's*. We are the great-grandparents of multi-generations of Powell's with more to come as time progresses.

I am reminded of the riotous laugher in Claire's den that turned my family's attention on me. "How are you doing, GG?" June asked.

"I'm fine, GGD. We are all so proud of you. And just look, you have new permanent front teeth coming in," I told her.

"We missed you when you went on vacation."

I had laughed. "You were having too much fun with your friends to miss me much." I knew Helen did not tell her children what really happened to me. Truth be known, I'm somewhat unsure myself.

There is no *we* for me and Thomas Kessler. I have not heard one word from him since mid-July when we said goodbye. I suppose it's for the best, considering our stormy relationship and illegal activities.

On the positive side, I've managed to worm my way back into the Friday Canasta Game, but only because my replacement decided she wanted to move to Ohio to be near her grandson. Lucky me!

I keep waiting for the other shoe to fall, but it doesn't. I am no princess with a lost silver slipper and no prince is coming to rescue me from boredom. It's all up to me to create an interesting future.

I glance around the Senior Citizen Center. Not many people have come out today for the luncheon. I wanted to play cards.

"You want to be Lorene's partner?" Jane Murphy asks me.

"Why wouldn't I? We've always been partners."

"Just thought a change would be good for you," she says.

"You think I'm bored?" My dandruff is getting up over her remark. "I am grateful to be home and all in one piece."

"We heard that CIA agent was sweet on you, Dorothy."

"If you call kidnapping me sweet, yes." I glared at Jane. Lizzy was always a gossip. However, I miss Tom and cannot help myself.

"We should sit down and play cards," Lorene suggests.

I take a seat across the square table from my partner. I cannot help but notice how Jane and Lizzy keep looking at each other—like they have brilliant news they want to share but dread doing so.

I push back in my chair. "Okay, gals! What's bothering you?"

"You haven't heard?" Lizzy chimes in.

I shuffled the cards so Jane will deal them first. We always draw straws to see you has the first deal. Silly, but works for us.

I twist my lips. "Heard what?"

"He's moved back to Columbia," Jane spurts as she gives each of us thirteen cards. It's a perfect deal, so her team gets 100 points.

They are ahead already. In news, too, I suspect.

"Who's moved back to Columbia?" I daftly ask.

Lorene lays down 2 red threes and draws 4 cards from the stacked deck. "Well, just lookie!" she lays down another 3.

One more red three and our team gets 800 points. I never understood why winning is so important in cards. You play them once a week, and no matter who wins, nothing much changes.

"Why, Thomas Kessler," Lizzy says. "He didn't call you."

I suddenly feel sick at my stomach and faint.

28

I OPEN MY EYES and see Arthur standing over me. The last thing I recall is playing cards with my buddies. Is this another dream?

"How do you feel, honey?"

"What are you doing here, Arthur? You're supposed to be dead." Let's lay out the facts and quit pussyfooting around the truth. I am so blame tired of time and circumstances playing tricks on me.

"It's okay, Dorothy. You've been in an automobile accident."

I try to connect the dots in his statement. "Do I own a Cadillac or red BMW or a navy-blue Audi 4?" Knowing will help me cope.

"Your old Cadillac, why do you ask?"

"How old am I?"

"You're being silly, Dorothy."

I glance around the predominately white room, reminiscence of the time I woke up in a hospital with Tom standing over me.

Was any of that real?

Is any of what's happening now real?

"What day is it?" *Dé j` vu*, all over again.

"April Fool's Day," Arthur replies.

"Well, that's better than Hell."

I actually chuckle, reminded of the Grand Cayman Islands and wonder if I'll land back there when time changes on me again.

"What are you talking about, Dorothy? You were in a terrible automobile accident eighteen months ago. You had a concussion. You've been in a coma until a week ago. Dr. Hammons sedated you, for obvious reasons." He intensively glares down at me.

"What obvious reasons?"

"Periodically, you have come to yourself and screamed about people and things that make no sense—inventions of your damaged brain. You've been checked over and everything physically is fine."

"In other words, I am in good health except for my confusion."

"Exactly." Arthur nods.

"Can I have a few minutes alone?"

"Sure, honey. This is a lot to cope with."

Tell me about it! I want to study my situation and decipher which part of my life is actually real and which part I've invented.

"Wait, Arthur! Is Claire here?"

"Down the hall, in the waiting room."

"Am I in Columbia or Nashville?" So many unknowns.

"Columbia General Hospital," he replies.

I nod. "Ask our daughter to come in."

He closes the door and a lovely woman enters.

Claire is prettier than I remembered. A few gray hairs are threaded in her fluffy ruby-red curls. Her Robin-blue eyes are huge and poignant. I want to leap out of bed and ferociously hug her.

But I am too weak.

"Mama! You scared the bejesus out of us."

She sits on the edge of my bed and grasps my hand.

"Did my Cadillac make it?" Ridiculous question, but important to me. "Did it?" I squeeze her hand.

"You were riding with Lorene."

"Oh." I think about those consequences. "Is she okay?"

"No, she isn't."

"How bad were her injuries?"

"We should talk about this later, when you're better."

"No, I want to know *now!* How is my best friend?"

"She died on impact. I am so sorry."

"What about Crawford?"

"He's devastated, of course. Graham married and moved in with him," Claire replies. "It is temporary while he builds a house."

I nod. At least, I got that right. I'm not all *that* crazy.

"Did Graham marry Dr. Cynthia Preston?"

"How do you know that, Mama?"

In a dream, I think, but that sounds crazy.

"Butch Peters and Ellie Simpson also married," Claire reports.

"Great!" I thought he died. I have no residual hard feelings.

"Anyone get killed recently in Columbia?" I inquire.

"Nothing much of note happens here in our quaint town."

That's the problem, I think to myself. That's probably why I invented such a bizarre scenario while unconscious to make up for boredom. Lorene always said I should write a novel. Maybe, I will one day, when the time is right. Right now, I do not want to think of never seeing Lorene again. A sadness comes over me.

"Do you want to go home?" Claire asks.

"The farmhouse?"

"Yes, where you've lived, like, forever."

"Sure. I'll need a wheelchair—oh, do we have a new director for the Senior Citizen Center?" This is a critical question for my sanity.

"Nope. Same ole, same ole guy is still running it."

Boring, I think, but I won't let that cat out of the bag.

"Help me sit up. I feel like my muscles are jelly."

"You'll need physical therapy, Mama. For a few days you will need bedrest. A therapist will come to the house three times a week to assist with your recuperation. Recovery will likely be slow."

That is not something I want to hear.

"Oh? Did I purchase a condo?"

"What makes you think that?" Claire's forehead furrows.

I only shrug, holding in a huge sigh.

"Okay then, I'll go down to the office and sign you out."

29

2nd Sunday in December

THE NEWSPAPER PRINTED an article about the elderly woman that miraculously survived a fatal accident. She had died for ten minutes, been revived, but was left in a coma for eighteen months. Dorothy Jean Powell was the talk of the town. A mystery to her friends.

The First Methodist Church of Columbia's senior Sunday School Class is in session and buzzing with the news. Elizabeth Hinson, especially. "She's a tough old bird," Lizzy spouts.

Charlie Bark is presenting the Bible lesson today since their regular teacher is sick with influenza. "No doubt she's a survivor."

"I bet she'll be back to playing Canasta in a month," Lizzy says.

"Should we send her flowers? I heard she went home yesterday."

"We'll take a vote," Lizzy decides. "All in favor?"

Charlie counts the hands.

"It's unanimous. Lizzy, will you order them for us?"

"Sure, my pleasure."

* * *

I am home, sitting up in bed when Arthur presents me with a bouquet of red roses with baby breaths. "From our Sunday School Class." He places the large green vase on the bedside table.

I have been crying all morning. Lorene's death is just hitting me. Arthur sits on the edge of the bed holding tightly to my hand.

"Honey, you cannot let Lorene's death destroy you. You must focus on getting healthy again." He smiles. "I love you so much."

"I love you, too, Arthur."

The trouble is, I'm still in love with a dream. I can see Thomas Kessler so clearly. He is Clark Gable, Matt Damon, and Bruce Willis all rolled into one. My dreamboat for all time. An invention of my demented mind while I was in a coma for a year-and-a-half.

"Here, let me dry your tears," Arthur offers.

I feel the soft tissue on my cheeks and wonder if I'll ever be the same again. Jesus once told me: *We are all in God's dream.* I don't understand time at all. Dreams seem so real. I could be in one now and not recognize it. All this makes me wonder if someone on another green planet looks through a telescope at earth, will they see only a barren rock? The thought scares me. Truly, I want to be sane.

* * *

"How is your mother, Claire?" Ted inquires as he affixes a tie to his blue shirt. He's lost thirty pounds and has been working out regularly at the gym. "Want me to go with you to Columbia today?"

"I think Mama would like that, Ted. I'll phone Helen and see if she'll go with us to the farm. Billy and June always cheer Mama up."

Claire slips on a long skirt with a winter-white sweater. Billy was baptized following the church service earlier this morning.

The trip south over to the farm takes almost an hour. Traffic has picked up in the afternoon around Cool Springs as Ted drives the family in his Mercedes Benz faster than Claire likes.

"What did the doctor say about your mother's mental condition after being so long in a coma?" He glances over at his wife.

"Physically, she appears fine. She's still upset over Lorene's death." Claire looks out the window at the snowdrifts in the bushes.

Arthur is standing on the front porch of the farmhouse as Ted pulls up in the circular drive. He waves for them on come on in, then goes inside the house. "Dorothy! The kids are here."

I am wearing the new robe Claire gave me, not feeling strong enough yet to get dressed. Arthur and I have been lounging around the house all day. I keep detailing in my mind how this house looked after it was repaired from tornado damage. Thomas Kessler was with me that day when the storm struck. I might redecorate my house.

"How are you feeling today, Mama?" Ted asks.

I love that he calls me Mama and not Dorothy.

"I'm getting better, still a little foggy in the noggin," I tease.

Claire sets a big white sack of Kentucky Fried Chicken on the table. The food smells heavenly and I'm hungry.

"Daddy, will you get us some sweet tea to go with our meal?"

"Did you go to church this morning?" I ask Claire.

"The early service, so we could bring you lunch," Ted answers.

"How sweet of you!"

30

"THANK YOU FOR COMING in for a consultation, Ms. Burkes."

"Claire, please." She takes a seat in front of Dr. Joel Sharra's spacious desk. "Is Mama worse?" Why else did he summon her?

"Actually, I have good news. Dorothy's responding to the new psychiatric meds—a combo of biogenically enhanced older ones—you might not understand the chemistry effects were I to explain."

"No, I probably wouldn't understand," Claire admits.

He thumbs through a thick folder of patient notes.

"As you probably read in the Columbia Chronicle, Dr. Robert Hammons recently passed, so I've been assigned to Dorothy's case."

Claire nods. "Do you have questions? Is that why I'm here?"

"Yes, you know your mother best." He points to the file folder. "Dr. Hammons made extensive notes of his sessions with Dorothy, and I've begun to systematically listen to his recorded tapes," Joel explains. "As you are aware, Dorothy has been diagnosed with a type of schizophrenia. Were there any earlier signs of mental illness?"

"Mama was always a bit paranoid and suspicious of others' motives," Claire replies. "She has a huge imagination and wants to write a book one day. When the time is right, she always said."

Joel makes a few notes on a clean page of his booklet.

"She majored in Biology but never finished college. She married Daddy and they lived in an apartment in Dickson."

"Anything special about the place where they lived?"

"Mama became close to a waitress, a woman named Lorita—she was Spanish, I recall. She rented next door to my parents."

"When did your parents decide to move to Columbia?"

"Lorita was murdered. Mama was so upset she said she couldn't stand to live there anymore. She cried until Daddy moved her. The newspaper reported Lorita's husband was involved with the Mafia."

"Back to an earlier time . . ." Joey reflects, "did Dorothy ever express regretting not graduating from college and becoming a teacher?" He pauses. "Disappointment can trigger depression."

"She never said," Claire reports, "but Mama is easily bored."

Joel nods. "It appears she is now a highly intelligent, functioning schizophrenic with a touch of dementia creeping in as she ages."

Claire nods with tears in her eyes.

"When did you notice her fear of going outside the house became worse?" Joel inquires, pen in hand as the tape recorder runs.

"During Mama's change of life, she quit going out with friends," Claire says. "I asked her why, and she said she was being watched."

Joel knows that's a sign of paranoia.

"Ted thought Mama should talk to a psychiatrist, so I contacted Dr. Hammons. He put her through a mental treadmill, then suggested treating her symptoms with antidepressants."

"But I see where you had her committed three years ago."

"Yes, after Daddy fell off his tractor down by Crystal Creek and almost died, Mama freaked out. She has not been well since."

"In what specific ways?" Joel asks.

"She believes Daddy was murdered and I cannot convince her otherwise," Claire says, wringing her sweaty hands, lips feeling dry.

"Even when she saw him in the flesh?" Joel makes some notes.

"She thought he was a ghost and panicked. Daddy moved out of the log cabin and we hired a private nurse. Lorene Perkins. She was great, more Mama's best friend than her caretaker. They were about the same age. Lorene played Canasta with her at the Senior Citizen Center every Friday afternoon. She loved Lorene very much."

"Do you think Lorene's moving away upset your mother?"

"Oh, yes, very much. She believes Lorene died in an automobile crash. They were riding together when it happened."

"Strange how the human mind operates when something goes awry." Joel shakes his head. "I had hoped your brother would come with you. I like meeting the immediate family to see how they react."

"Lance and I are close, but Mama wrote him off when he began long-hauling for a vegetable company out of West Tennessee. She fussed at him about eating too many fattening burgers while on the road—it would cause him to have a heart attack." Claire falls quiet.

"You said Dorothy wrote him off, how is that?"

"She thinks he died from a heart attack when he turned fifty-one." Claire shakes her head. "It freaks her out to see him, so he doesn't visit her anymore. We agree that is for Mama's best."

"Dr. Hammons made a note that your mother once climbed upon a stool and leaped off. She claimed she was pushed from an airplane by a beautiful young CIA agent named Kelly," he says.

"I don't know anything about that," Claire reports.

"I am going to address all of these issues with your mother now that she is more lucent. Would you like to be present to verify some of the things she tells me?" he inquires. "She must distinguish between reality and fantasy if she's to ever function in society again."

"Yes, please."

"I will email you a list of issues I want to touch on so you can be prepared to comment during the session," he tells Claire.

"Thank you. We want Mama well and back home."

"Oh? What about the farmhouse? She went on and on about the repairs following a tornado. Do your parents still own it?"

"No, they never did. Mr. Clyde Willems does. He was a Texas oil guy before he bought the farm and moved into the house."

"Strange that she insists owning the property."

Claire doesn't know how to respond.

"What did your father do before he retired?"

"He was a field agent for the Tennessee Forestry Association. When Daddy retired, he began working for Mr. Willems, tending the cattle," Claire explains. "My parents lived in a log cabin three miles behind the farmhouse." What stories has her mother been telling?

"Does Dorothy realize your father passed last fall?"

"I hope so. We let her scatter his ashes over the cow pasture he loved so much tending to," Claire reveals. "Please help my mother."

Joel smiles. "I'm doing my best, Ms. Burke."

"Claire, please."

He shakes her hand and they part.

While Ted is waiting outside the mental hospital for Claire to return, his daughter Helen phones. "Hi, Daddy. Where is Mama?"

"She's talking to your grandmother's psychiatrist," he replies.

"Let me speak GG." He hears June scream.

"Put the little pumpkin on," Ted says.

"How is GG doing?" June chuckles. "Is she having fun?"

"I'm sure she is," Ted replies.

"June, give me the phone," Helen says.

"Daddy, tell Mama to call me when she has an opportunity."

"I will, sweetheart."

"I want a full report on how my grandmother is doing."

"Will do." Ted ends the call as Claire returns to the car.

"Is she better?"

"I hope so, Dr. Sharra seems competent and has put Mama on new experimental meds. We're hopeful she'll soon return to reality."

* * *

"It's time for your new meds, Dorothy."

I look up and see a handsome man, fifteen years younger than me. "I'm a little foggy this afternoon. Remind me of your name?"

"Clint."

"I love the name Clint. Howard, isn't it?"

"Yes, I'm your floor nurse." He smiles at the patient.

"I promise not to tell your secret," I whisper.

"What secret is that?" Clint knows but he plays the game with Dorothy anyhow. Living in a fantasy world helps her cope with incarceration. When his shift ends later tonight, he can go home to his wife Kelly, but Dorothy will be stuck in this locked lonely room.

I motion with a finger for Clint to come closer.

"I know about the Thomas Kessler thing."

He chuckles. "Of course, you do. Keep our secret?"

"Only if you promise not to kidnap me again."

"With all my heart." He crosses his chest with a finger.

"Oh, bring me that book on the shelf with the words circled in it." He knows which one. "I must keep it close to me and safe."

Clint crosses the room and plucks the children's book from the shelf with dozens of books featuring photographs and descriptions of interesting places around the world that Dorothy Powell will likely never visit. She is particularly fascinated with the Middle East and talks about the clandestine banking industry thieves cater to.

"This one." It is a children's book: *The Secret Garden*.

"Yes, that's *our* book, Clint."

He never understood what she meant by that.

"I used to sit and read it to my son Lance when he was a boy—he died of a heart attack some time ago. Claire liked the book, too."

"Your daughter," Clint says. "Here, drink some water and take your meds, dear. I still have my rounds to do."

"Okay, Tom." I wink at him. "Will you come and see me tomorrow?" I grab his wrist. "Promise to come and see me again?"

"Wouldn't dream of not coming, Dorothy."

He watches the patient swallow the pills with water.

"I wish you didn't have to go, Tom."

"Clint, please. Remember our secret?"

"Oh, of course. Silly of me. Have a nice day, Clint."

31

CLAIRE IS STILL upset as Ted drives his gray Mercedes Benz to their home in Brentwood. "Did the doctor explain how these experimental meds for schizophrenia work?" he inquires.

"He believes the meds are helping her think more rationally."

Skeptical at the diagnosis, Ted remarks, "Look, honey, even if your mother improves, we cannot put our lives on hold for her. I don't want to cancel our flight to London and lose my deposit."

It was something Claire always wanted to do.

"It's a wonderful idea, Ted, but the timing may not be the best."

"There will never be a good time where your mother is concerned. We're paying big bucks for the hospital to take care of her." He gets his angst up when Claire puts her mother first over their needs. Dorothy never thinks about anyone but herself.

"Don't be mad. We may be able to swing it," she says.

"I want more assurance than that, Claire. I have to arrange for my partner to take over my business while we're away three weeks."

"Three weeks!" Claire ekes. "You know I want to go, but I can't be gone for that long." She blows her nose. "If Mama is not better by then, I don't see how I can leave the states. She depends on me."

Ted doesn't like Claire's answer. He's skeptical that any kind of new meds can change the course of Dorothy's life. Claire cannot keep playing the role of a mother to a mentally-sick parent. It isn't fair to her or him. He shakes his head, disgust in his expression.

"Don't be mad at me, please!" Claire pleads. "You know I cannot depend on Lance to look after Mama. She's already paranoid that something will happen to us. She's like a frightened child."

"Exactly. It irks me she's constantly complaining to you about our relationship." He will have his say about his mother-in-law.

"She doesn't recognize the truth, Ted. Give her a break."

He slams the pedal with a foot and speeds up the car. As soon as they are inside the house, he goes into his office and slams the door, effectively shutting Claire out of further discussion about Dorothy.

"How is GG doing, Mama?" Helen asks Claire over the phone.

"I didn't get to see her, but I spoke with her new psychiatrist."

"What about Dr. Hammons?" Helen asks.

"He recently passed, so Dr. Joel Sharra replaced him. He reports Mama is slowly improving on some new experimental meds."

"Does that mean they are not FDA approved?"

"Probably, but I agreed with him that trying something different was better than letting your grandmother live in a fantasy world indefinitely," Claire says. "I want her well. I love my mother."

"We all love Grammy and pray for her every day."

"I hope one day soon she can come and live with us."

"You and Dad?" Helen huffs. "He'll never agree to that."

"Then I'll buy her a condo close to us, here in Brentwood. I cannot imagine Mama living out the rest of her days in a mental institution, or that awful log cabin your granddaddy purchased."

Helen is saddened to the core over her mother's distress.

"Do you think mental illness runs in our family?"

"Oh, Helen, I hope not. Mama did not show symptoms of schizophrenia until she was well into her seventies."

"I hope you're right. So far, Lance and I appear to be normal and we're well into our fifties. God would not be so cruel."

Claire is silent on that subject. Genetics sometimes seem to play a greater role in humanity than God's intervention with mercy.

"We just have to be patient, Mama. You know God is good."

* * *

Dorothy sits staring into space as Dr. Joel Sharra begins his fourth session with her. He's connected a device to her head that reads out on a monitor the pattern of how her braincells fire.

"What day is it? I don't have a calendar." I look at him.

This is good, Dr. Sharra thinks. The patient has made eye contact for the first time this week. The meds are helping.

"What about my calendar?" I demand an answer.

"We gave you one on Friday. Where did you put it?"

"No, you didn't. Or I'd have it," I tell him.

"Let's talk about something else. I'll get you a new calendar."

"Okay. What do you want to talk about?"

"How do you feel today?" Dr. Sharra asks.

"Fine—did anyone follow you here?"

"Why do you think someone followed me, Dorothy?"

"Don't call me that. My name is Daphanie."

"Okay, Daphanie. Why do you think someone followed me?"

"I'm not in good standing with some bad folks."

"What bad folks?" Dr. Sharra turns on the recorder.

"I stole some money from Russians peddling dope to our kids."

"When did that happen?"

"I don't know. Maybe recently. Maybe a long time ago," I answer. "Sometimes I get confused. Time changes on me, but that's not important. My safety is. I may be called to testify against them in a court of law. They know that. Those drug lords are unforgiving."

"How does that make you feel?" Dr. Sharra inquires.

"Terrified that they will find me, shoot me, and kill every member of my family," I explain. "My friends are not even safe."

Dr. Sharra takes a moment to note the response in writing.

"You don't believe me," I say.

"Do you know where you are, Dorothy?"

"I'm right here, talking to you."

"No, what is this place where you live?"

I look around my room and see so many things that belong to me. "Home, I believe. Why do you ask? Are you one of them?"

"No, I am no threat to you, Dorothy. I am your friend. I am a doctor trying to help you see what is real and what you think is real."

"I don't want to think about all that. It depresses me."

The patient's head falls forward. She is sleeping, or in a catatonic state. Who knows what's going through her thoughts?

≈

It's spring again and I am aware that a stranger is watching me. Is this the Russian Mafia after me again? I know Detective Chico reported to Claire that Danny Mason was behind Zoey Jackson's death, originally believed to be a suicide. He also tried to kill me, but Gloria Bolton drank my latte instead. I haven't seen Gerry since I returned home from the Grand Cayman Islands. I hear he left town.

What a shame! We were becoming good friends.

Despite my rift with his third wife, Gerry understood my side of the story. Gloria and I were rivals in high school. I despised that she dated my husband Arthur first. When she moved back to Columbia, I could not help disliking and distrusting her. My bad.

Poor Arthur—murdered by that insane Mark Hagen.

I did not want Gloria to die from ingesting a poison meant for me. But better her, than me—I know that's selfish, but it's self-preservation. Everyone must feel like that. I pray Jesus forgives me.

Isn't that what God's grace is for?

Forgiveness for many errs.

I am seated in my Audi 4 outside of Lorene Perkins' house waiting for her to come out and go with me to the Senior Citizen Center. We will have a nice lunch first, then play cards with Lizzy Hinson and Jane Murphy. Jane never liked me. She tried to replace me with one of her friends, but I will never let her.

This is my Canasta Club!

"Have you been waiting long, Dorothy?" Lorene asks as soon as she opens the car door. "Graham called and I got sidetracked."

"Only a few minutes. You look really nice today."

"Thank you. You, too. I'm thinking of getting a facelift."

"I've inspired you. Good. But, unless you start dating again, you'll be wasting your money." Let's be honest here.

"You think Tom is coming back?" Lorene makes a face. "He's off on another CIA assignment. You need to be real about him."

I only shrug. Lorene doesn't understand true love.

"I heard you've written your first novel draft based on your international escapades," Lorene remarks. "I'm proud of you."

"I'm not going to end the book until Tom returns to Columbia. He asked me to marry him, and I've decided to accept."

Lorene's eyebrows lift as her mouth falls open.

"You're surprised?" I speak. "You know how much I love him. Arthur would want me to be happy for the rest of my days on earth."

"I want you to be happy, too, but you are fantasizing, Dorothy. Thomas Kessler has used you to accomplish his purposes. Face it, he's through with you." She smacks her lips and I almost hate her.

"I forgive you because you are my best friend."

≈

I wake up, as if from a dream. "Who are you?"

"Dr. Joel Sharra," the man dressed in medical whites replies.

"Are you related to Dr. Lyle Sharra?" I inquire.

"He was my uncle."

"He performed surgery on my face—that's why I look younger. I'll soon be eighty-three," I inform him.

Joel clears his throat. "Remind me of your birthdate?"

"1939," I respond.

"That makes you eighty-five, Dorothy."

"You are mistaken, Dr. Sharra!" My angst is up. "I always mark my calendar to keep up with the days, months, and years."

He waves a hand. "It's not important, Dorothy."

"It is to me." I nearly shout. "I know how old I am."

He does not answer me. I am in no mood to talk to him anymore. "I want to go home. I should not be here."

"Do you know where home is, Dorothy?"

I think about his question. "I don't."

"This is a private mental hospital."

"Are you a patient?"

"No, Dorothy. You are."

At his words, I feel faint.

32

Four Days Before Christmas

CLAIRE WANTED TO KNOW more about schizophrenia so she Googled the site for information. There were several forms of the mental illness identified by psychiatrists. Some patients exhibited only mild symptoms while others lived out their lives in a fantasy world.

Dr. Joel Sharra believed that her mother's condition fit *paranoid schizophrenia*. Hallucinations, hearing voices others didn't, and false beliefs that conflicted with reality. At times her mother appeared to be sleeping or in a catatonic state, which meant she could not be wakened. Schizophrenics had difficulty thinking and responding appropriately in a normal manner. They might forget or misplace things. Pace or walk in circles when agitated. Failure to have eye contact when spoken to, or the desire to feel important in their own eyes. Traumatized, Claire shuts down the computer and weeps.

* * *

I stare at the Christmas tree in the corner of my room. The door is locked and I feel safer. Clint locks it every time he leaves after giving me my night meds and tucking me into bed. I know Lorene thinks he doesn't care about me, but she's wrong. He's moved back to Columbia and assumed his former identity as Clint Howard—just to be near me, and to keep me safe from both the CIA and the Russian thugs. Claire, on the other hand, wants me to come home.

Not my home at the farm, but her house in Brentwood. That will not happen. If I decide to leave my safehouse it will be with Clint. He has yet to ask me again to marry him, but I know he still loves me. Or why else would he stick around an older gal like me?

I hear the door lock click and it startles me. *Clint?*

The door swings open and I see my son Lance standing there.

"Mama, I came to bring you a Christmas present."

I point at my son. "You're not real, you're dead!" My heart is palpitating and my skin is cold and clammy. "Go away!"

"Mama, it's me, Lance. Don't you recognize me?"

I look at him. "Come closer and let me touch you."

He puts a beautifully wrapped gift on the bed and approaches. I reach out and take his hand. "You feel real. Are you really here?"

"Of course, I'm here, Mama"

"I can't be sure, Lance. I get all mixed up. Where are we?"

He smiles. "You are in a hospital getting better."

"Better from what? Do I have cancer?"

"No, you just need to rest and get better."

The door opens again and a tall man dressed in white enters.

"Good afternoon, Dorothy. Lance," he greets my son.

"You know my son?" I am surprised.

"Yes, we've had a nice talk about you, Dorothy. Now that you are better, he wants to take you to your daughter's house for a visit."

"Better from what?" I feel confused. "Have I been sick?"

"Yes, but not physically," he replies, extremely pleased with the progress Dorothy has made toward recognizing her situation.

"Am I crazy?"

"No, just confused, but you're getting much better," he says.

I think about Clint and if I want to leave the safehouse.

"Mama? Do you want to come with me to Claire's?"

I look at the doctor for advice. *Should I?*

"I can sign you out for a week, Dorothy—if you promise to take your meds everyday as prescribed. What about it?"

I look at Lance. "What about Clint?"

He looks at the doctor for an explanation.

"He's Dorothy's floor nurse."

I think to myself Clint Howard is so much more to me than that.

* * *

We are in Lance's SUV when he phones Claire.

"I have Mama checked out of the hospital and we are on our way to your house," he says. "Want to say hello to her?"

Lance hands me his cell phone.

"Hello. Is this my Claire?"

"Yes, Mama. I'm so pleased you'll be spending the holidays with us. The kids are coming over on Christmas Day to visit with you."

"Helen and Benjamin?"

"Yes. Helen's children have grown since you've seen them."

"Are you talking about June and Billy?"

"Yes. June is seven and Billy is nine years old now."

I try to remember what they look like and can't. I give Lance his phone back. He says to Claire, "Mama doesn't want to talk anymore." Then ends the call. "You doing all right?"

"I think so." Some distressing details of my life are coming into focus. "Is Arthur dead?"

"Yes, Mama. He died last year."

"How old am I?"

"Eighty-five."

I nod, feeling sad. "Did he die from a fall near Crystal Creek?"

"No, his heart was weak. He passed from lung cancer."

I recall he smoked a lot when he was younger.

"Are you telling me the truth, Lance?" I don't know what is real anymore. My doctor says the meds are good for me, but are they?"

"Of course, I'm telling you the truth, Mama."

Still, I wonder if anything going on around me is real.

* * *

I wake up and my doctor is staring at me. We are in my room again. He sits at the table across from me. He's drinking hot tea.

"I thought I was in the car with my son Lance," I tell him.

"No, Dorothy. You've been asleep sitting up."

"Tell me, is my son Lance alive?"

"Yes, he is. He wants to come and see you soon. I told you that yesterday. Did you forget?" He smacks his lips.

"I get confused—my memories are foggy sometimes."

"I know they are, Dorothy, but you are getting better. Do you remember what you were dreaming about just then?"

"I do." I describe how Lance came into the room and signed me out for the Christmas holidays. "We were on our way to Claire's."

"Excellent! We're making real progress!"

"Are we?"

"Yes. Do you want to visit Claire and spend Christmas day?"

"Does she want me to?" I return. I am safe here. I don't know if I will be at Claire's house. The Russians might be watching her.

33

Christmas Day

I AM IN CLAIRE'S Buick riding on I-65 toward Nashville. Bing Crosby is singing "White Christmas" over the radio. Snowfrost is on the bushes alongside the interstate. "Is it going to snow today?" I ask.

"Later today," Claire replies. "I've arranged with Dr. Sharra for you to spend the night," she tells me. "Is that okay with you?"

"Sure. Why wouldn't it be?" I think about the day. "I didn't get anyone a Christmas present, Claire. Will they be upset?"

"No, of course not. I bought a few things for the family and attached your name to the wrap," she says. "I hope that is okay."

"What did you get for them?"

"Well, for Helen and Patrick, I purchased two tickets for the live theater downtown. *Little Annie* is playing and I thought they'd enjoy a night out away from the kids. Ted and I will keep Billy and June."

"That's nice," I say. "And for Billy?"

"He's big into sleeping overnight with his friends so I purchased a new camouflage tent that four can snugly occupy," she replies.

"And June?"

"A Disney doll with a set of clothes—she'll love it."

"What about Ted? He doesn't like me," I say.

"You're wrong, Mama, Ted loves you."

"Did I get him sticks and soot because he's been a bad boy and cheated on you with other women?" I chuckle. "Scratch that."

"Mama! That was mean. Please don't start a fight with him."

I throw a hand. "Oh, I won't. If he doesn't with me." I like to finish my own arguments and win. That's why the Russians have never caught and punished me for working with Tom and stealing their drug stash. I suddenly want to hear his voice. I'll call him.

"Aren't you going to ask me what you got for Lance?"

"I can't talk about my son; it makes me too sad."

"Mama, Lance did not die from a heart attack. He still works for PicSweet and drives vegetables to market," Claire explains. "He's coming for dinner and bringing his girlfriend, Freida somebody."

"You don't even know her last name? Isn't Lance a little old to still be dating? He should be married and have grown children."

"I bought Lance a Walmart gift card from you."

I don't comment, and I do not want to see Lance.

Silence captures me the rest of the way to Claire's house located in Brentwood. Five cars are parked in her driveway. Too many people. Thinking about answering their questions about my health scares me. "Claire?" Will she take me back if I ask her?

"What, Mama?" She pulls into the garage, closes the door, and shuts off the motor. "Don't even think about skipping out on us."

Us? My family? I suppose I'm doing this, like it or not.

We get out of the car and Claire retrieves my overnight bag from the trunk. I follow her inside the house like an obedient child.

"Merry Christmas, GG!" shouts greet me from the den.

"Merry Christmas!" I repeat back and feel a black veil slowly sliding over my vision. Before I know it, the room turns black.

* * *

I do not know where I am. I am standing alone on a deserted beach. The ocean waves crash against the rocky shoreline and leave the sandy soil embroiled in white foam. The sound is deafening.

"Dorothy?"

I turn around and smile. "I should have suspected."

"I've been looking for you for a while," Thomas Kessler says as he approaches. "Where have you been hiding?"

"I was locked up in a safehouse, Tom. A man that looks like you—his name is also Clint—he keeps watch over me."

"Clint Howard?"

"Yes, that's the name he gave me. But he isn't you."

"No, he isn't me, Daphanie. What do you want to do today?"

"Where are we?"

"The Grand Cayman Island," he replies.

"Hell?"

He snickers. "Yeah, I never understood why the natives called it by that name—this is a paradise. Both for vacationers and thieves."

"Which are we today?"

"Visitors."

"Should I remind you that you've kept the money Charlie stole from the Russian mob?" I say. "That fits the description of a thief."

"Except you're dead wrong."

I do not like that word. *Dead*.

"Prove it to me, Tom."

He smiles. "Don't you trust me?"

"I want to," I admit.

"You must." He grins. "Love binds. Don't you know that?"

"It sure has bound my heart into a knot." I suddenly feel chilly. I look up in the sky and see a waterspout forming. "We should go."

"Where, Daphanie? Where can we hide that no one can find us? You have to know they will take you away from me," he declares.

"How can anyone take you away from me? It's your choice if you want to be part of my life. I don't ever want to lose you."

"But you will, Dorothy. You will . . ."

He fades away as the waterspout rakes the shoreline. I have no choice but to run. I do not want to die here on this lonely beach.

***

I open my eyes and see Ted standing over me.

"Where is Tom?" I ask as I sit up. "Did I just faint?"

Then I notice Claire standing beside him.

"You've been, uh, out for a few minutes," she explains.

"By out you mean I fainted?"

"Yes. Are you okay? Do you need to take one of your meds?" Claire asks. "Dr. Sharra said you might need an extra antidepressant from time to time—seeing coming here might be a bit traumatic."

My family, all of them, are in Claire's den—just staring at me. I am the center of everyone's attention and I don't know how to react. What can I say? I don't want to be here. I want to be with Tom.

34

January 2

I AM BACK AT the safehouse and feeling more at ease than when I was visiting Claire. My daughter means well, but she does not understand my need to be among friends—not that I don't love my family, I do. It's just that they make me feel uncomfortable.

The door to my room opens. I wait to see if it's Clint and wonder if I should confront him about his tricking me into believing he is my Tom. But it's not my nurse, it's Dr. Sharra.

"Good afternoon, Dorothy. How are you today?"

"I'm fine." I stiffen. "How are you today, Dr. Sharra."

He chuckles. "Good. You recognize me." He drops in a chair at the table where I have most of my books open.

"Anything interesting in those?"

He refers to my picture books.

"A great deal. Did you need something from me?"

He grins, then plucks a book from the pile entitled Middle Eastern Mysteries. "Did you find anything useful in this book?"

"A few magic potions I'd like to try on you," I tease.

He laughs hard. "You seem so much happier today, Dorothy. Did you enjoy your extended visit with family?" He'd decided to let the patient remain in her daughter's care since she was doing so well.

"It was enlightening," I reply.

"In what ways?"

Always probing my thoughts.

"My greatgrands have grown and changed so much."

"Were you happy there?"

"Actually, this place feels more like home."

He makes a note in his booklet.

"Oh, thank you for my new calendar. It helps me keep the days and weeks straight." I have another birthday coming up in June.

Old enough to croak, but I don't want to think about dying.

"Your daughter mentioned you wanted to write a book," he informs me. "Would you like a laptop computer so you can begin?"

"I have already begun," I respond and show him a pile of notes I stowed in a cigar box—which I have no idea how came to me.

"Writing by hand can be therapeutic, but easier on a computer."

"Maybe for someone as young as you are," I return. "I'm not sure I know how to use one." Let's be bluntly honest.

"I can arrange for someone to teach you the ropes."

"They have ropes on a computer?" I am teasing.

"Your decision." He's not giving up on my becoming more modern. Doesn't he know you can't teach an ol' fool new tricks?

"Okay. I'll give it a try."

We talk a few more minutes about what I enjoy. This session feels pretty good. More positive. Or maybe I'm less negative about how life will turn out. Dr. Sharra seems to understand me better.

"Let's talk about your dreams." He shifts the subject.

"What about them?" They are private and I prefer to keep it that way. I have enemies and I don't know if Dr. Sharra is trustworthy.

"Would you like to know your diagnosis?"

"What do you mean?" I squint my eyes at him.

"I'm talking about why you've been kept here, in this room, for almost three years." He changes the tape on the recorder. "Do you?"

"Do I what?" I'm not sure I understand his meaning. The unknown scares me. Doesn't diagnosis refer to a physical ailment?

"I must warn you that what I am about to say may prove upsetting," he utters. "But if you are ever to live on your own, you need to understand your problem." He shifts in his chair.

We stare at one another for a long moment.

"Okay, I'll play your game. What's my diagnosis?"

"You are mentally ill, Dorothy. A paranoid schizophrenic with the onset of dementia," he tells me that with a straight face.

Hell's bells! I want to clobber him.

"Exactly, what does all that mean?"

"It means you often believe things are happening to you that aren't. You slip into a dreamlike state and live in a fantasy world that helps you cope with reality." He probes my face for a reaction.

When I say nothing, he pipes, "Do you understand?"

"Oh, yes . . . what you are saying is I'm insane."

"There are degrees of insanity," he clarifies.

"That doesn't make me feel any better."

"The meds are helping you get well," he explains. "In time, you may live on your own. Or with Claire. At some point I may release you as a hospital patient. With additional therapy, of course."

"What about Thomas Kessler and that other female agent—Kelly somebody?" I recall her nickname. "Drop-Dead Gorgeous."

He winks a smile. "They are figments of your imagination."

"Clint Howard isn't. He moved to Columbia to run the Senior Citizen Center—Oh, I don't know, I forget exactly when."

"Clint is your male nurse. You invented him as a CIA agent."

"Well, Lorene Perkins is certainly a real person!" I nearly shout.

"Yes, she is. But she was your caregiver when you became ill right after Arthur's accident—after he fell off a tractor in the cow pasture by Crystal Creek. You believed he died, but he didn't."

"Arthur is still alive?" I am shocked.

"No, he passed last year from heart and lung problems."

This is a boatload of information that seems farfetched to me.

"I don't believe you," I tell him. "You are part of them."

"By *them* you refer to the Russian mob. None of those clandestine things you believe is true has happened, Dorothy. I know all this is shocking. But I want you to think about what I've said."

I feel faint. I hate this man. He is not my friend.

"Wake up, Dorothy!" Dr. Sharra shakes her, but she's sleeping.

* * *

I am once more on the sandy beach. *Hell*, I think. The whirlwind that picked up Tom has dissipated into a dusky blue sky. The sun will soon be setting. I don't like the darkness. I am alone and miss Tom. I rest on a rock and stare at the white-foamed ocean waves.

"Tom, please come back to me. Don't let them take you from me!" I cry out to the ocean. "You were so right. I cannot trust anyone but you." A deep sadness swallows me as the day turns darker and dreary. Thunder rumbles in the distance.

It's going to storm. Where can I find safety?

35

A Week Later

A LAPTOP SITS on my desk. I stare at it like it's my enemy. It feels like a snake that will bite me if I touch its rattlers. Claire was here yesterday and showed me how to turn it on. Good for her.

I stare at the blank screen, afraid to switch it on.

The door to my hospital room opens. I spin around in the ergonomic office chair Ted gave me as an early birthday present. It's a long time till June, but he's trying to be helpful.

"Good morning, Dorothy. I have meds for you."

I smile at Clint Howard. He's so young and good looking. No wonder I like him so much. He could be Tom's twin brother.

I swallow the four tablets and drink half a glass of water.

"Anything you need before I go?" he inquires.

"Yes, will you help me get this fandangle thing going?"

"Oh, the laptop!" He laughs. "Sure, no problem."

Clint is a whiz at modern communications. The iPhone he carries around with him has his daily schedule recorded on it. There's also a monthly calendar and a camera if he wants to take a picture. I can't imagine how anyone came up with so powerful an invention.

"There you go! I opened up the Word program for you."

"Claire told me all I have to do is start typing."

"Easy as eating pie." He grins.

"I won the typing award in high school. Still this computer is a far cry from a Royal. Claire said it even corrects misspelled words."

"Spellcheck." Clint points to the icon. "Don't let the computer spook you. It's a good friend. In time, you'll love it."

I love a lot of things, but I doubt it will ever be this thing.

"Okay, I'll leave you to writing your book."

"Claire told you." I glare at him. So much for secrets.

"No, Dr. Sharra mentioned it. He believes recording your thoughts will be helpful to your recovery."

I know he's referring to my mental illness.

"Well, I gotta make my rounds."

"Oh. Tell Kelly hello for me."

I hear the lock to the door click. I am alone. Just like as always. But now I have a new friend. My computer. So, I start typing. I begin when Arthur went to feed the cows on October 24th, nearly six years ago. I'm telling my story like I experienced it. People will call it fiction, but I know better. Who can better describe my life?

≈

Clint brought Dorothy's lunch to her. She's sleeping with her head lying on the table in front of the laptop. The screen is blank.

He touches her shoulder.

"Huh?" she sits up. "Oh, Clint."

"Dorothy, it's lunchtime. Want me to remove your computer from the table so you'll have room for your tray?"

"Yes, thank you." I try to focus my eyes.

"I see you did not write anything this morning."

"I did." I know I did. "Someone erased my work." I become upset. "It's *them*! Those damn Russians! They don't want me telling their secrets." I grab a wad of typing paper and begin shredding it with my own two hands. "I could kill those bastards! I hate them!"

"Calm down, Dorothy. You'll hurt yourself."

I am so angry I jump up from my chair and tip over the table. My tray of food scatters over the floor alongside a glass of tea. Before I know it, Dr. Sharra races into the room and looms over me.

"I'm sorry, I'm sorry, I'm sorry . . ." I am weeping.

I feel a needle stick my arm.

"Calm down, Dorothy. You need to rest now."

≈

As I fall asleep, I stand in front of the precinct where Detective Lloyd Peters once had an office. Once inside, the officer checking in people nods at me as I walk to the elevator. Jake knows I'm a regular.

Upstairs, I open the door to Detective Galena Chico's office without knocking. Her male secretary sits at a desk, typing something.

"Is Detective Chico in? I need to see her."

Hands drop from the computer keys. "I'll check."

"Uh huh. Yes. Okay." Blake ends the call. "She'll see you."

The door comes open. "Come on in, Ms. Powell."

If this were Butch, he would refer to me as Dorothy. Our feud for decades had eventually evolved into a mutually-uncomfortable friendship. Ellie had helped forge that bridge. Before Butch was shot and burned in his apartment, I had almost forgiven him for molesting my Claire when she was in the ninth grade. He came from an abusive home and has done relatively well as an adult—considering his violet upbringing. I have only one goal in mind today: solving murders.

"Thank you for seeing me," I remark.

"Have a seat, Ms. Powell," Galena says.

I take a seat and glance around. Looks exactly the same.

"How may I help you today, Ms. Powell?"

"Dorothy, please." I clear my throat and lean forward in my chair. "I hear Danny Mason is in custody. I want to see him."

"You're talking to the wrong person, Ms. Powell. Captain Colbert needs to sign off on a visit to the Maury County Jail."

"Can you at least tell me if he'll be prosecuted?"

"We know he's guilty of murdering Gloria Bolton and Zoey Jackson," she reports. "He's admitted to committing the crimes."

"So, he'll be executed?"

"I don't know if that will happen."

"He'll cut a deal with the police!" I am belligerent. "People who do terrible things never get punished. It's the way of politics."

"Seems that way," she reluctantly admits.

"I need your help, Detective Chico. Please."

A moment passes between us.

"I need to ask him why he killed Zoey."

"Okay, I'll talk to Captain Colbert and see if she'll schedule a visit for you with the creep. I hope that will give you some closure."

"I'll never get over Zoey's death. That beautiful girl had so much promise. You know I was paying her way through college."

"Yes. Mighty nice of you."

"Her jailbird daddy wasn't going to help her. Zoey's granddaddy did his best to care for her, but with no mother in the picture . . ."

"I'll phone you when Captain Colbert has set up an interview for you, Dorothy. Is there anything else I can do for you today?"

"No. Thank you." I leave the building and drive away.

≈

When I wake up from my nap I am lying in bed. It is dark in my room. The shade to my lone window is pulled tight. It is night.

I glance around my room and recall the mess I made of my lunch tray hours ago. The floor has been wiped clinically clean.

The last thing I recall is a needle going in my arm. Dr. Sharra gave me a sedative because of my rage. I cannot recall what set me off. But I know Clint was here. He brought my lunch.

I've lost time again. Did I actually talk to Detective Chico about Danny Mason, or was it all a dream? It is becoming more difficult for me to separate my two lives. I wish, in a way, I could have both.

Mental illness will do that to a person, I am told.

My stomach rumbles. I feel hungry. I missed supper. They can't starve me in here; it must be against the rules. I should demand that someone feed me. I am becoming upset all over again.

I have a bell on my desk, so I ramble over and give it a ring.

A nurse I do not recognize opens the door. "You called?"

"I missed my supper. May I have something to eat?"

"Sure." She starts to close the door.

"Wait! Who are you? I don't recall you working here."

"I just started. Tonight is my first shift."

When the door is closed, I think about who this woman might be. Has the Russians sent her in to watch me? They cannot keep me from telling the truth about all the bad things they did. I intend, with God's help, to write what happened to me when Tom kidnapped me. I will expose CIA Charles Darby for his crimes against the USA.

Where is Tom? I really need his help.

36

Four Months Later

IT'S LATE MAY, a beautiful spring morning. I'm staying with Claire for the next month. Dr. Sharra says it's to see how I function under normal circumstances in the real world. What does he know?

I'm on mental probation. If I'm a good girl, I'll get to live on my own. But if I don't take my meds regularly and lapse into dreams, I'll need to return to the hospital for more treatment. So far, I'm doing pretty good. I've come to grips with the fact that Thomas Kessler is a figment of my imagination. I don't like it, and I'll miss him terribly.

He's like a character in a good novel. But pretty real to me.

Best he can, Dr. Sharra has explained to me how my quirky mind works. When Arthur fell off his tractor and hurt his head, I believed he was shot by a Russian assassin. I invented a western-wild series of events to explain why he left me alone to survive in this world until my time was up. After my mental breakdown, Claire hired Lorene Perkins to stay with me at the cabin while Arthur recovered from his head injury. When Lorene Perkins quit her job and moved away, I missed her so much I created a friend I could trust with my life, tell everything, and play Canasta with every Friday.

To me, Lorene was my best friend and next door neighbor. Like me, she lived on a farm with her husband Crawford. He died soon after my Arthur—a heart attack, they'd reported. But I suspected he was the victim of a serial killer, scared to death by Mark Hagen.

To a normal mind, the story I invented would not make a lot of sense. How can one woman get into so much trouble? Hadn't my fictional characters said that all too often? But to a functioning schizophrenic, the world I invented was all too real and frightening.

Today, I am riding in an Uber on my way to Columbia where I intend to clarify some *real* details in my mind. My first stop is the farmhouse where I believed Lorene resided. Of course, her husband Crawford had to die like Arthur since I needed a strong connection to her. We were soul sisters in our suffering. She had my back.

Claire paid for the ride here, so I thanked the driver and got out of the car. I'll call for another Uber driver when I'm ready to leave.

I stand in front of a house that looks exactly as I remembered it in my dreams. It is a two-story house with white clapboard siding, dormer windows, and a green metal roof. A lovely property.

I bravely mount the front porch, tap on the front door and wait. A young woman opens up and stares at me. "Ms. Powell?"

She is young and beautiful and I'm envious. My lips seem sealed. I want to ask to speak to Lorene, but I know she never lived here. I need to see who really does. "I, uh," keep stammering like a fool.

"Can I help you with something, Ms. Powell?"

"Dorothy, please. Remind me of your name?"

"Cynthia Perkins. Dr. Cynthia Perkins."

"The Maury County coroner, right? You are married to Grant. Do you have a baby?" I am on a roll to decipher the truth.

"Not yet." She smiles. "It will be a few more months."

Well, at least I'm not all that crazy.

I don't have an invitation to come in yet. Cynthia's heard about my mental breakdown and is afraid of me. I understand. Dr. Sharra told me to expect that kind of response. Still, it bothers me.

"Would you like to come in for a visit?"

I look past the beautiful young wife and spy Grant Perkins. He is just as I remembered him in my dreams. He has a younger brother, Sam. A firefighter, I believe. I've been here many times before.

"Thank you, I will come inside for a moment."

We walk through the foyer into the den. The kitchen is to my right, as it was when Lorene lived here. There is a spacious bar.

"Cyn, fix Ms. Perkins a cup of coffee," Graham says.

"Sugar and cream?" She looks to me for an answer.

"Yes, perfect." I glance around the house. The furniture in the den sits in the exact place as I recall. These people know me.

"Is your mother here, Graham?" I get right to the point.

"Yes. She has a cold and is sleeping."

I need to see this woman—just to make sure she isn't the Lorene I envisioned in my dreams. But I do not want to contract a virus with my birthday coming up in early June. Claire has a party planned.

"Graham? Do we have a visitor?"

I turn around and am shocked. Alicia Colby stands there.

"Dorothy. How nice to see you again," she tells me.

"Good to see you again, too." I am bowled over. How in the world did I confuse Graham's mother with the elderly woman from Manchester, England? Alicia is several years younger than me.

"I, uh, just wanted to stop by and say hello," I utter. I don't think we were all that close before my breakdown. But we are neighbors—it makes sense that I'd include her in my fantasy world.

The four of us sit at the dining table enjoying cups of hot cocoa laced in bubbling marshmallows. I ask a few questions about my hometown; how Columbia is progressing in the modern world.

Graham tells me Cynthia is expecting a baby soon. In my visions, she'd already given birth to a little one.

"A boy?" I inquire.

"Yes, good guess."

"Yes." I smile. "A good guess."

Our visit ends thirty minutes later.

Graham offers to drive me to Clyde Willems' farm—the house I believed belonged to me and Arthur for most of our married life.

"Thank you," I tell him, "I'm not driving myself yet."

"Good to see you doing so well, Dorothy."

"Thank you, Alicia. A lot of people have prayed for me."

Have they? Am I a good Methodist?

The drive is brief. I get out of Graham's car and tell him I can take it from here. Clyde's red BMW sits in the driveway.

I chuckle to myself. In my visions, I owned that car.

Clyde may be sleeping in oil money, but he looks like an ordinary farmhand. His hair is too long at the neck and the deep wrinkles embedded in his tan face reflects a lot of outdoor time spent on this farm. Perhaps that's why I placed him in that role when Arthur and I owned this house. I've always been jealous of his wealth.

Isn't coveting a sin? I have to do better.

"I heard you were out of the hospital," he tells me.

"Yes, I wanted to come and see you. To thank you."

"Arthur and I were close. You got my potted plant?"

"Yes." I don't recall what it looked like. Then I think of the plant from Hell, Grand Island that I mailed to Lorene Perkins.

In my visions, of course. "Were the blooms big and red?"

"Yes, it was a plant from an island I once visited."

Makes sense now, I think to myself. I've confused real life events with my schizophrenic visions. I've been all mixed up.

"I'm going to miss Arthur. He knew my cows like the back of his right hand. Never was there a more clever poker player."

"Arthur sure loved his Friday night outings."

Clyde motions me to a barstool at the breakfast bar in his remodeled kitchen. After a series of tornadoes raced across Middle Tennessee, one took the roof off this house. A tree crashed through the den. A true fact, I believe. Which means I was inside this house before the damage was repaired. Lorene brought me here.

"Have you moved back to Columbia?" Clyde inquires.

"No, I'm homeless. Claire sold the log cabin. I don't know the people that bought it. I've been staying with my daughter Claire in Nashville." I won't mention I'm still under psychiatric treatment.

Clyde grins at me. "I'm so proud of you, Dorothy. Arthur would be proud, too, if he could see how well you are doing."

I'm silent on the matter, wondering what else we have in common to talk about. Nothing. We have nothing in common. He was Arthur's boss, not the other way around. I was impoverished.

I must have had a desire to be rich, even famous. I needed to somehow lure Thomas Kessler to find me. I would be useful to him. He was madly in love with the smart, beautiful double-agent for the CIA. He married Daphanie Daniels but she was murdered by a Russian assassin decades before we met. I had to look like her.

Because I wanted to become her.

Daphanie was the only person capable of stealing Russian drug funds stashed away in international banks. Tom would come to love me as much as he did his deceased wife. Then, I would no longer be alone after Arthur died, and later when Lorene Perkins left me.

Odd how the human mind works. It's complicated.

"Can I get you something to drink, Dorothy?"

"No, thank you. I had hot cocoa at the Perkins' house."

"Honey, who's here?"

I turn around and am overcome with shock. Ellie Simpson stands there. "Dorothy! So good to see you."

"When did you and Clyde get married?" I inquire. And wonder if Lloyd (Butch) Peters ever dated her. I knew him as a youngster.

"Last year," Ellie replies. "You look well."

"I'm trying to put my life back together." Humpty Dumpty never made it. "Visiting people I know helps me sort things out."

Little I believed to be true is fact. We talk about the drought seizing Middle Tennessee and I ask about how people at First Methodist Church are faring. Ellie and Clyde are members in good standing. I suspect that I am not. And that must trouble Jesus.

37

AN UBER DRIVER takes me back to Claire's house. It's late in the day by then. Ted is home early from the office. "Hi, Mama."

He calls me that because he knows I don't like him.

"Hi, Ted," I say back. After all, I am under his roof—not that the house is not half Claire's. "Did you have a productive day?"

"Did you?" Claire asks, her feet propped upon the coffee table.

"It's hot in here," I note the temperature. "Is the AC out?"

Ted snaps his feet to the floor. "We have a guy coming tomorrow to fix the unit. Are you hungry? Claire made sushi."

I hate raw fish. "No thanks, I had a burger on my way home."

A small white lie, but I suspect I've told much bigger ones when I was out of my mind. I don't know why I am condemning myself. Maybe it's because the story I invented is not true. And Tom will never return to me. We will never marry and live happily-ever-after.

"What did you do today?" Claire clears away the clutter and magazines from the coffee table so Ted can serve us cold drinks.

"Thanks." I accept a Sprite.

"I visited the Perkins' house," I answer. "Then I went over to Clyde's farmhouse. We had a nice conversation. Ellie was there."

"Oh, yeah," Ted chimes in, "I heard he married her."

I take a seat in the wingback and look at my daughter. "What ever happened to Butch?" I take a quick swig of my Sprite.

"Who?" Ted plops down on the sofa beside Claire.

"Lloyd Peters," I answer.

"Why, Mama, I haven't heard that name in decades."

I look at Claire. In my visions, before he was murdered, he was the lead detective in several murder cases unfolding in Columbia.

"You knew him in high school, right?"

"He was a prick," she scowls.

"Did he once try to molest you?" I inquire.

I have Ted's attention. "I never heard anything about this."

"Aw, honey, it wasn't worth mentioning," Claire remarks to Ted. "He felt me up and down one day at the school bus stop."

"I'm sorry I didn't protect you from that," I tell my daughter.

"Mama, you could not have known it would happen."

"After Lloyd graduated from high school, do you know what happened to him?" I need more clarification.

"I don't know. You can Google his name."

"I'll help you with that," Ted offers.

"We waited supper on you, Mama. Are you sure I can't fix you something? I knew sushi is not your favorite food."

Ted glares at me. "I didn't know, Mama."

"It's okay, Ted. You and Claire have a nice meal. I want to go to my room and lie down. I need to think about my day."

"Your meds are on the bedside table," Claire calls out to me as I tromp down the hallway to the guest bedroom.

I look at the four bottles of pills and ignore them. I need a nap. And I want to see Tom again. The meds keep him from me. That is unacceptable. But I cannot let Claire know I'm missing doses.

God forbid that Dr. Sharra find out!

I am with Charlie Darby. We are on a large motor boat racing around the long sand-lined coasts of the Grand Caymans. This is my chance to find out more about Daphanie Daniels, and why he and Tom were less than friends while working together for the Central Intelligence Agency. "I see questions in your expression, Dorothy."

"Call me Daphanie—which makes me wonder what she was really like." I want to bait Charlie so he'll be brutally honest with me.

He laughs. "She's not you, that's for damn sure!"

"But I look like her—Tom said so. Have you forgotten I walked into four banks and moved the money Daphanie deposited in 1991, plus every dime you put in the account since?" I am on a roll.

"No, I have not forgotten. And you will get my retirement stash back for me," he says. "Or I promise you won't be breathing."

"You don't scare me, Agent Charlie! Death is stalking me at my age. I'd rather die than help you with one single, little, tiny thing!"

Now that's telling him!

"Daphanie had more charisma than any woman I'd ever met when she walked into the CIA office in D.C. I fell head over heels in love with her," Charlie recalls. "She was older, but I didn't care."

I was older, too, and Tom didn't care.

"But she liked Tom better," I egg him on.

"He never trusted Daphanie."

"Because she was a Russian agent," I say.

"Yes. I suppose Tom told you I was groomed by the SVR to snoop for them in America." The look on his face spells hate.

"I know. Tom and I have no secrets between us."

"I don't want to talk about Daphanie anymore," he says.

"You murdered her because she married Tom," I say. "If you couldn't have her, nobody else could. And she changed."

"Yes, she changed. I knew she would double-cross us," Charlie rants. "Daphanie had no idea I was a double agent so that made it easier to fool her. All I had to do was say I had valuable information that would help solve a case. She came to me like a bee buzzing to honey. I shot her in the head and watched her die. It was the highlight of my CIA career. And it devastated Thomas Kessler."

≈

I stir from a deep sleep as a hand touches my shoulder.

"Mama, wake up!"

I sit up. "Oh, Claire." I glance around and the bedroom is dark. It is night again. "How long have I been sleeping?"

"It's ten o'clock. You didn't take your meds." She holds out her palm with four tablets. The other hand has a glass of water.

"Oh, I didn't. Sorry." I swallow the dadgum pills.

"You should get dressed for bed. I'll be in our bedroom if you need me through the night," Claire says. "I love you, Mama."

"I love you, too, Claire."

38

3rd Friday in May

ELIZABETH HINSON WAS in Nashville for a doctor's appointment Friday morning, so I bummed a ride with her back to the Senior Citizen Center. Where else can you get a lunch for five bucks?

"We've missed you at the Center," Lizzy pipes from the driver's seat. She is driving a five-year-old Chevy the color of dark chocolate.

"I've missed all my friends, too," I say, although it's not true.

"Are you out of the hospital permanently?"

I look over at Lizzy. "Nothing in life is permanent."

"Well, uh, I know that—I just meant. . ."

I interrupt her thought. "You just meant, am I well?" I do not say crazy. Dr. Sharra warned against using that term. It has a bad connotation. Normal people are easily frightened of the mentally-ill—not that I'm not getting better. Hey, give me a second chance.

"I don't want to hurt your feelings, Dorothy."

"I know you don't, Lizzy. And I do appreciate my Sunday School praying for me while I was, uh, under the weather." This conversation is getting more difficult by the moment. I need to redirect the subject matter. "How is the Center doing?"

"What do you mean?" Lizzy passes a truck on the interstate.

"I heard we have a new director—is that true?"

"Oh, yeah. Gerry Bolton and his wife moved back to town."

This is getting weird. I wonder if I am dreaming, or is this really happening to me in the flesh? "Who did Gerry marry?"

"Gloria Ann Lake. You went to high school with her, right?"

"Right." I grit my teeth. "Did she ask you about me?"

"Yes. Just how are you doing? Have I seen you lately? What was your problem?" Lizzy goes on with a few other scenarios.

"What did you tell her, Lizzy?" I am smoking at the gills.

"That you were under a doctor's care." She lifts her hands from the wheel and the car swerves. "Promise I did not say mentally ill!"

"Don't wreck the car, Lizzy!" We narrowly escape an accident. The driver behind us bears down on his horn and scowls at us.

"Sorry," Lizzy apologizes.

I can tell she is upset. Tears cloud her lime-colored eyes.

"It's okay, honey, I have to deal with my illness. And others will need to be patient with me," I tell her. "I'm not dangerous."

"We know you're not."

We incorporates a lot of territory. Folks who know me in my hometown. My church members and friends I associate with. Every blessed person residing in Maury County who reads the newspapers.

How can I overcome the stigma of craziness?

Lizzy is through trying to make conversation. It's for the best. I have nothing more on the subject of my illness to contribute. After a forty-minute ride she pulls into the parking lot of the Center.

"Thanks for the ride, Lizzy. I catch an Uber from here."

"Aren't you coming inside for lunch?"

"I have an errand to run first." I exit the car.

She hops out the other side and calls across the hood, "Don't you want to say hello to Gerry and Gloria?"

"It's early yet," I reply. "My errand should not take too long. I'll be back by one. I'd like to say hello to the Canasta gang."

"Okay, I'll tell Jane and Beverly."

Beverly Trenton. I thought she'd moved away some time back. Jane never liked me. She's been trying to replace me for as long as I can remember. But Lorene and I were a team. *In my visions.*

After Lizzy went inside the Center, I walked a city block to the Columbia Police Station. I wanted to speak with Captain Marilyn Colbert—just to make sure nobody has been murdered in our quiet community in the past three years. I'm sweating by the time I arrive.

The building that houses our law-enforcement team of officers has stood solid for nearly a hundred years—a landmark downtown. The lobby is just as I remembered it. I sign the register then request an interview with Captain Colbert. The officer on duty frowns.

"What?" I lean into his face. "Do I have egg on my face?"

"No." He reviews the appointment book.

"I don't have an appointment, but would you call up to Captain Colbert's office and ask if she'll see me?"

His gaze is a bit skewed, like he's looking down at his own nose. He reads my name on the roster and glares a moment.

"You are the Dorothy Powell?"

I do not like the part about "the." It has a negative connotation.

"All day long." I tap my right shoe on the tile floor.

"Have a seat over there." He points to a bench. I am not optimistic I will get an interview with the Captain today, but it is worth a try. I want so badly to sort out the truth affecting my life.

Yesterday's copy of the *Columbia Gazette* rests on the other end of the wooden bench. I scoot over and fling it open to see what headlines the front page. ENERGY PRICES SURGE.

Nothing new there! I toss it back where it came from.

A black frumpy woman wearing an official police uniform steps off the elevator and walks toward me. I stand up to greet her.

"Did you want to see me?" Captain Colbert asks. She has a no-nonsense presence about her that commands immediate respect.

"Yes. Do you know me? Have I been to see you before?"

She winks a smile. "I know of you, yes."

"Then you know I've been in a mental hospital for almost three years," I tell her to verify what she probably already knows.

"Why don't we go for coffee? I was about to take a break."

"Sure." I pick up my Walmart special and trail her out of the building. Coffee Call is a block away, across the street from the Maury County Courthouse. The clock in the tower says it's 11:35 a.m.

"I need a sandwich with my coffee," the captain says as soon as we are seated at a compact table for two. "What will you have?"

"A hazelnut latte," I reply. "Let me buy you lunch."

"You don't need to do that. Let me get your coffee."

We could sit here all day arguing over who will pay for her lunch, a coffee, and my latte. I don't think it's worth our time.

"All right, as long as the next time I treat you."

She smiles. "That's a plan."

The waiter takes our order. He looks nothing like Danny Mason that served me my "latte to die for" in my vision of a different kind of existence. It's shocking to see Gloria Bolton walking our way.

"Captain!" she hails then looks at me. "I heard you were out."

I want to crawl under the table.

"Gloria!" I try to sound cheerful.

"Am I interrupting something official?"

No, I'm not under arrest, I want to say, but instead forge ahead with, "I heard you married Gerry and moved back to town."

"Yes. Last year. I'm picking up four dozen pastries for our dessert at the Center," she remarks. "Lizzy said you might drop by."

"I plan to, if time allows." I'm ready to end this uncomfortable confrontation. We never liked one another in high school and nothing has changed. Why even make an effort to be friends?

"Okay, have a nice lunch!" Gloria is off to the races.

Captain Colbert glares at me. "Do I sense bad vibes between you two ladies?" She is brutally honest and I cave.

"I'm afraid so—can we talk about something else?"

Our coffees arrive and the latte is beyond delicious. I realize I have been deprived of so many simple pleasures while hospitalized.

"Dr. Sharra is my psychiatrist," I begin. "He wants me to visit the locations and talk to the people I interacted with during my schizophrenic episodes." I know no better way to state my reason for wanting to meet with the captain of the police force.

"Call me Marilyn," she says and I know we are communicating on a friendship level and not one that's professional.

"Thank you, Marilyn." I take in a huge breath. "Evidently, I invented a new life for myself when I believed my husband was murdered nearly five years ago. Did you know my Arthur?"

"We never met personally," Marilyn replies as her ham sandwich arrives. She bows her head for a quick blessing.

"That was nice," I comment. "God is good."

"Yes, He is. Go on with your story, Dorothy."

While she eats, I summarize what I believed had transpired since Arthur's accident—his murder by a hired Russian assassin. Crawford Perkins was next on the list since he knew about Clyde Willems' gambling problem and had lent Clyde money. Zoey Jackson's grandfather was Mark Hagen's next target, then much later, Danny Mason murdered Zoey Jackson, making her death look like a suicide.

Captain Colbert does not comment. But her dark eyes reveal her disturbing conclusions to my radically impressive fake story.

"I know, it's hard to believe," I comment. "Detective Lloyd Peters took the lead on these murder investigations," I finalize.

She sits back in her chair and wipes her lips with a napkin.

"I'm told none of that happened. It's the figment of my imagination, interspersed with visions and catatonic states."

Marilyn pushes back her chair. "I don't know Peters."

"I'm told he never moved to Columbia."

"All of this must upset you very much."

A tear drips down one cheek. Tom does not exist either.

I lean forward. "Did any of this ever take place?"

Marilyn shakes her head. "Not to my knowledge."

"Who is your lead detective now?" I have to be sure.

"Galena Chico—she transferred from Miami."

I release a sigh. I got that right somehow.

"Thank you for your time, Captain. I should go now."

I'm up and on my way to the door when Marilyn calls after me, "You know . . . you should think of writing a novel."

I smile and wave at her and laugh. "I've been told that."

* * *

A city cab carries me out to the log cabin where Arthur and I once resided. Pete and Marie Brown own the property. They are real people, so I wasn't all that crazy when I placed them in my visions.

Marie answered the door. "Oh, hello, Ms. Powell."

"Am I interrupting anything?" I glance around the cabin. It looks as it did before the elderly Alicia Colby remodeled it.

"No, we've had lunch. Pete went over to Clyde's to take care of a few chores that needs doing," she answers. "Come on in."

"I will, thank you."

"Can I get you something to drink?"

"No, I just had a coffee in town. Do you have sons?"

"Yes, two rowdy boys. They are at school right now."

"Do you mind if I see my bedroom?"

"No, of course not—we heard you were released from the hospital," Marie says as she leads the way to a small bedroom.

"I'm living with my daughter now."

She splays her hands. "The place hasn't changed much."

Marie walks over to the compact closet and retrieves a hat box from the top wooden shelf. Then faces me.

"You left this behind."

"What is it?" I take the floral box the size of a large cake and shake it. Then I put my ear to it. "Making sure it's not a bomb."

Marie laughs. "The box wasn't mine, so I didn't open it."

"Can I take a peek now?" I rattle it again. Very light.

"Of course, it must be yours."

I set the box on Marie's bed and flip open the top. Inside sits the exact Gucci purse Tom purchased for me in Paris, France.

"You don't look well, Dorothy. Sit down."

I nearly fall back on the bed. *Is this real?*

39

AN UBER DRIVER RETURNS me to Claire's house in Brentwood by mid-afternoon. All I've learned in Columbia prompts me to believe I'm crazier than I first thought. The hatbox throws me, though.

How did I come by such an expensive item if Tom did not give it to me? I go straight to my bedroom to think about everything.

A tap comes at my closed door.

"I'm resting, Claire."

"Don't lock the door, Mama. Please."

"Okay, when I get up, I'll unlock it."

"Let me in, we need to talk."

"No, dear, I need to rest."

"I do not want to knock down the door."

Double S-S! "Okay, I'm coming."

The meds still sit on the dresser I did not take this morning. Claire methodically counts them out. "Okay, I didn't take them."

"Mama!"

"You don't understand, honey. I don't like the real world. I don't like my life. I want to live in my fantasies. They make me feel better. More alive. More purposeful. Like my life really counts!"

Claire looks like I've slapped her.

"Sorry, but the truth needs to come out!" I exclaim.

"Okay, calm down. Let's talk about your day. What did you learn in Columbia?" She hands me a cup of water with the meds.

I have no choice but to swallow them.

"I had coffee with Captain Marilyn Colbert at Coffee Call. Gloria Bolton was there getting pastries for the Senior Citizen Center," I begin. "I learned I still cannot stand the woman."

Claire actually chuckles.

"Is any of that real?"

"I don't know. You tell me."

"Will you phone the Center and see if Gerry Bolton is the Director?" I request. "Reality and fantasy go together. . ." *Like a horse and carriage*, I recall some old song lyrics that make me smile.

"What do you mean, Mama?"

"What is true? My vision of life, or an alternate version?"

Claire pats my hand. "I'm sorry, Mama. I know you are trying to sort out your life. Ted and I just want the best for you. If you do not take your meds regular, you may have a relapse."

"I know that. Would you send me back to the hospital?"

"I'd rather not, but you need to stay on the meds," she declares. "Your freedom is on trial. What happens to you depends on you."

Now there is a prophetic statement if I've ever heard one.

Sleep comes to me around ten p.m. I had a nice supper with the happy, normal couple then excused myself to read a novel. I like Lee Child's JACK REACHER books. They are full of macho excitement.

The novel lies on my chest as sleep captures me . . .

≈

I am seated in the meadow not far from Crystal Creek. This is where the drama all began—where Arthur fell off his tractor and hurt his head—where Mark Hagen had murdered him. It is a pleasant spring afternoon. The daisies are blooming. Green grasses stand tall. Butterflies flit among the foliage, avoiding the buzzing of honey bees.

This is where Thomas Kessler said goodbye to me. I try to recall his voice and what was said before he left me forever. I should have told him I'd marry him while I had the chance. I am a foolish woman. I pluck a four-leaf clover and suspect luck will evade me.

But I am drop-dead wrong.

"Dorothy!"

I turn around, astounded at seeing him.

"Tom!" I rise to my knees. "You came back for me."

"Of course, I did." He walks toward me.

I smell his cologne. I want to grab him and never let him go. His grin melts my heart to its core. "Why are you here?"

"Now that's the sixty-thousand-dollar question."

I cannot help but laugh at his stupid antics.

"How long will you make me wait for an answer?"

"How long do you have?"

We are playing a foolish game for lovers.

"Okay, I give up. Now?"

"You should know I've retired from the CIA and am back for good." He kneels in the grass and a diamond ring glitters in his palm.

"Yes, I'll marry you! Yes!" I fall into his embrace and every dream I've ever had—every wish, every desire, they all come true.

"Before we marry, there is something you should know."

"What is it, Tom?"

Do I really want to ruin the mood of this moment?"

"The CIA has tricked you, Dorothy."

My mind whirls to make sense of what he's said.

"What does that mean, Tom?"

"The pills you've been taking have made you crazy so you would believe our clandestine trip overseas never happened," he explains.

"Does Claire know that?"

"No, but Dr. Hammons was in on the ruse."

"So, we really did rob banks and go to Hell?"

He chuckles. "We really did, Daphanie Daniels."

M. Sue Alexander

About the Author

M. Sue Alexander has been penning her thoughts since early childhood. She is a graduate of Bolivar High School in Tennessee and earned a Bachelor of Science Degree from Union University in Jackson, Tennessee in 1962. For decades her attention was given to writing songs while working as a public-school teacher, and later as a real estate sales agent in three states. Her first novels were penned in her early forties but she did not publish until 2003 when the first book in her *Resurrection Dawn 2014* series was uploaded to Amazon Books. The *Crystal Creek Mystery* series was Sue's inspiration after she turned eighty. Deciding older women needed encouragement to view a more exciting future, Dorothy Powell became the epitome of hope for her readers. This series is both funny and serious, sometimes preposterous. The storyline points out the mental, emotional, and physical hoops older women must leap through to achieve happiness.

Share vital information

Help your vendors do their job by sharing critical data with them. Sales, conversions, specials and new product and service data give them material to work with. The act of sharing information breeds trust and common accountability to shared goals. It also helps protect against a vendor hiding bad performance data or covering up mistakes.

Practical tips

Here are some other ways you can leverage your vendors experience and expertise:

- Learn how to read analytics yourself and ask detailed questions about your traffic and conversions.

- Get some of your internal people Google-certified so they can understand what the vendors are doing and ask better questions. This is not very hard or expensive, but gives you a big edge in the long term.

- Make sure that bi-weekly or monthly calls are happening and that your team comes prepared with specific, well-thought-out questions.

Stay Connected at the top

The final recommendation we have for you is to make sure you talk to the CEO of each of your vendor companies at least once a year. Tell them about your experience with their team as well as your goals for your business going forward. Ask them what thoughts and experiences they can share about your market or general trends that might be affecting you. Simply scheduling

Power Questions:

- "What can my team be doing to accelerate your work?"
- "What would you recommend we do more of if you had access to my team's time?"
- "In what way can our team be more involved in the online marketing campaign so this campaign has a higher chance of success?"
- "What things can we be doing on a monthly basis to complement your efforts?"

Working to absorb best practices and industry knowledge from a vendor not only improves the campaigns you're working on with them in the short term, but also helps to retain that knowledge in your organization after the vendor is gone.

Create a team mentality

When you finalize an agreement with a new partner, begin integrating them into your team. Build communication cycles that involve them in your internal planning calls. Treat your account manager at the vendor company like part of your staff and get them invested in the outcomes you're trying to drive. When they commit to doing something with your entire team, you can be sure they will give it a high priority. Remember that people work to make money – but they work harder when they feel accountable to people they like.

Here are some good open-ended questions to ask your vendor partner when you talk with them:

Power Questions:
- "What are the best practices for this type of work?"
- "What are you seeing that is working with your other clients?"
- "What trends do you see emerging in the last couple of months that are relevant to our business?"
- "What do you think we could be doing to increase our conversions?"
- "If you were in our shoes, what would you be doing that we aren't yet?"

Leverage

We often see CEOs leaving their vendors on an island. They believe that the vendor is responsible for obtaining certain results, but don't really put effort into using their own resources to increase the level of activity. In the case of online marketing companies, it is very often the case that a client will be paying for a defined amount of work to be done every month - content, page revisions, campaigns created, etc. If you adopt an approach geared towards leveraging your vendor's intelligence and your own resources, you can start asking questions like:

Hard Truth Number Seven: Even great partners need to be managed

As the owner of the business, it is ultimately up to you to create integration between internal resources and contractors. How well you do this has a big impact on the leverage you get on the dollars you invest in online marketing services. Here are some thoughts and best practices we've built around integration.

Communication loops

There are two communication loops you need to establish with an online marketing partner:

- A regular, scheduled call to review reports and discuss upcoming activity. This call should include your internal marketing staff – and your staff should be prepared with questions.
- Direct, impromptu communication via email and phone directly between your staff and your vendor account manager when new products/services are launched, changes are made to the website or seasonal specials or events take place.

The account manager you're working with probably has at least a dozen other clients and has a unique point of view about best practices in different areas that are relevant to you. They also work with a team that has even more clients, so they have exposure to a lot of different practices and ideas that could potentially benefit you. That's a lot of information which you could get just by asking. Most people don't ask.